ONE STRANGER'S SONGS

Christine Schonewald

iUniverse, Inc.
New York Bloomington

One Stranger's Songs

iUniverse books may be ordered through booksellers or by contacting:

iUniverse
1663 Liberty Drive
Bloomington, IN 47403
www.iuniverse.com
1-800-Authors (1-800-288-4677)

ISBN: 978-0-595-49668-6 (pbk)
ISBN: 978-0-595-49403-3 (cloth)
ISBN: 978-0-595-61201-7 (ebk)

Printed in the United States of America

iUniverse rev. date: 1/21/2009

Thank you each,
Rose for Louis
Bob for Dominique
Gabrielle for Jacqueline
Emelie for Hans
Louis for "Home"

Preface

Everyone has a history. Mine starts in Paris, where I was born in 1950. My mom met my Danish father in France; they married, and the rest goes on. I was about five and a half years old, when we immigrated to the United States. At that time, I only spoke French. Though, English came quickly at that age, thanks to television's old cowboy westerns and cartoons.

In San Francisco, where I grew up, I would often find myself surrounded by people speaking new languages, whether it was at the market, on the bus, or near school (downtown). I would hear the melodic sounds of Cantonese, Japanese, Italian, Spanish, Russian, German, and more. It was fun imagining what people meant when they spoke something other than French or English. I would fill in all between minds and hearts. That, together with my grammar school's Latin masses and our Danish Sunday services, fascinated me. I sang, filling in "no-meaning" sounds here and there to accompany beautiful music. I could not foresee how, many years later, I would come back to spilling words out as I listened to music after brain surgery.

As I grew up in the mid 1950's and 1960's, the city fed my fascinations non-stop. While young, I spent considerable time after school at ballet classes, the basketball court, my mom's office at the California Academy of Sciences' museum, or the student section, also at the museum. Despite this good life, I was doing poorly in grammar school and classed as "slow" on entering junior high. It makes sense that during high school my mind was barely academic. Basketball and field trips with friends were the priorities. My councilors told me not to bother applying for college. Dyslexia was not as easily identified as today; a poor student was simply defective. Remarkably, despite the academic setbacks, my parents consistently encouraged me regarding college. This support mad a tremendous difference when my migraines and partial seizures began later.

My freeze-dried-food cooking paid for innumerable backpacking trips and those adventurous climbs of my first high Sierra peaks, Mt. Darwin and Split Mountain. After rather poor scores on college entrance exams, junior college helped train me to slow down and be more careful as I read, and it opened my eyes to additional subjects: poetry, philosophy, physics, and art history. Two years passed quickly and I transferred, eventually graduating from the University of California, Davis. Finally, my graduate years were spent at the Smithsonian Institution's National Zoological Park and University of Maryland. Those years in graduate school were all fascinating ones. I spent my time studying mostly animal ecology and social behavior.

After finishing graduate school, I began working with the U.S. Marine Mammal Commission, the Smithsonian Institution's Natural History Museum, and for fun I performed with a Scandinavian folk dancing team. I taught for a year at George Mason University one year and, soon after that, worked with the U.S. National Park Service and joined the adjunct faculty at the University of California, Davis.

During the 1990's a number of great years came to halt. The effects of my divorce, the 1989 earthquake in San Francisco, my father's death, rebuilding my parents' house, my mother's cancer, and my daughter's struggle with Lyme disease were overlapping. Also, work became increasingly difficult. Several parts of my life had collided as 2000 approached. My health declined. Seizures and chronic Lyme disease were pulling my body apart.

I left my work and chose to undergo brain surgery to cure my epilepsy. Fate would decide if I would become normal. How the ensuing six years reversed sadness to joy, pain to pleasure, and passed by so quickly is amazing.

In order to reorient myself and determine what I could do after surgery, I decided to look back at my old notes. I wanted to review what had happened over the last forty years and imagine how things had come to where they were. The notes were to be the best sources for answers, so that's where I began searching and read my new and old notes.

Stacks of boxes were in the tool shed, full of squirrel winter-stashed acorns and mouse nests made of shredded book pages and covers, laboratory and field notes, and manuscripts. It is there where I exhumed most of the remaining poetry that would end up here, in *One Stranger's Songs*.

Truly, despite some obstacles, I've been a romantic and idealist my first half-century, and I'll retain that predisposition for this next half. Life had me listen for its sounds; they started me writing. Sometimes, communication requires a mix of descriptions, including joy as well as hurdles and despair to underscore the immeasurable value of options, opportunities, and hope. Thus, *One Stranger's Songs* retraces moments that contributed to that hope, as well as to my amazement and sense of humor.

I learned something new about the origin and contexts of my writing while I compiled *One Stranger's Songs*. Certainly, my verses were spawned by the mix of languages, childhood imagination, and an infusion of rhythms, word sounds, and music into life. The malleable attributes of poetry provide me a free, safe, and private passage to expression. While prose, especially technical writing, often suffocates me, writing poetry lets me breathe.

Poets are my tenacious "lifters." Writing poetry has done the same and lifted me. I started writing before I learned about style, and did not feel constrained. In retrospect, more form might have been a good thing. One certainty regarding any quality in *One Stranger's Songs* is the strong influence of the great music composers and poets whose works crossed my path. I am very grateful for their insights and influences.

Thus, *One Stranger's Songs* comprises my last forty years' writings. My desire is to present a slice of what has crossed time.

The first chapter of poems, "Life's Observable Time," is an assemblage of my different subjects and styles; it gives shape to what I've written. The chapters that follow compliment this first set of poetry, each representing a theme. None of the poems in this and other chapters are chronologically arranged.

Chapter 2, "Age," refers to my daughter and children in general, as well as the older, ageless people.

When my daughter turned six, while outside having fun in the coastal range, we found a tick on her and pulled it out. Not long after, a donut-shaped red circle appeared on her skin. My mom and I, being biologists, went to the books. We found and read about what we were seeing. Obtaining treatment was hell, without exaggeration. It wasn't until five years later that we found competent help.

Both here and in the chapter titled "Health's Sanities and Insanities," I express my feelings about my daughter. I express love and my continuous feelings of helplessness regarding her struggle with Lyme disease and how it affects her schoolwork, sports, social life, and worst, her self-confidence and -esteem. That, coupled with the lovingly typical and thankfully passing mortar exchanges between teens and moms, leaves me amazed that we've made it through. Fortunately, we had many good times to remember with some bad times intertwined, despite all. Love and humor persisted and health seems to now resurface after 22 years. Two months of daily hyperbaric pressure treatment seem to have finally restored her health.

We experienced especially the good and peaceful times. One memory regarding poetry returns to my mind often.

One day after work, when my daughter was about seven years old, I was tired of reading the same books at her bedside at night. I went to the Davis public library to find some children's books. That day, I couldn't find anything that gave me that motherly melodic inspiration, and I moseyed over to the poetry shelf. I must have wanted a poet's song. I swept my fingers over the shelf's textured bindings with my eyes closed. One worn book caught my hand. The book and one of its singular poems remains a classic.

Wallace Steven's poems became regular nightly bedtime "story-songs" that I would read aloud while laying my young daughter down to sleep. One of my favorites, very effective at getting her to sleep, was "The Man with the Blue Guitar" from 1937. My daughter's eyes would shut and her long lashes rest, peacefully, after only three or four stanzas. Then I couldn't help but continue reading aloud. Both the child's sleep and the poem's sound dismissed any stresses I felt. The process was as euphoric as anything I feel when engaging in endorphin-producing exercise.

Chapter 3, "Health's Sanities and Insanities," presents the hurdles of pain. The chapter focuses on the sorrow of illness and death of my closest friends and family members. Of course, it focuses on me too.

Some setbacks are klutzy accidents with only short term effects. Some do deserve poetry. Mine involved a case of coral poisoning, bone breaks, and cuts (like accidentally sitting on a pair of scissors). There are also the long-term and lifetime setbacks we experience. During my first fifty years, these took their time, perhaps so I could grow wiser, though the process seemed slow. A lifetime of dyslexia[1] and epilepsy, lasting chronic pain, nearly thirty years of ongoing Lyme disease, and a painful professional end all provided their challenges.

One by one: Dyslexia encouraged me to write poetry and increased my sensitivities to sound and rhythms rather than just letters in words. Epilepsy pushed me into an exploration of alternative means for problem solving. It also gave my perceptions flexibility, curiosity, and humor, which I hope to never lose. The chronic pain was caused by a fall[2], yet it taught me to write while mentally stuck for twenty years, due to painkillers killing pain, or overdoses of powerful painkillers during my late twenties, when I no longer cared that I was in pain. (This was before I started experiencing addiction and fortunately stopped.)

Chapter 4, "Metal Wings," is straightforward. It represents the incessant wait for "Boarding time" and "We're preparing to land" that we all experience

---

1   My dyslexia (for lack of a better term) involved the sequence of sentences and pages. I still can't see repetitions or notice sequence, and more. Just this preface required some thirty drafts. We all have our setbacks.

2   I had just climbed and descended one of the peaks in the Evolution Basin and was shooting to start my ten peaks above twelve thousand feet to achieve mountain climber status. Then having taken off my boots and put on plastic (not rubber) sandals, I rock-hopped on a glacial moraine's polished boulders, not looking where I jumped. The photograph I was taking of the mountain took my eyes off my last jump, which ultimately, along with moving East, cut off any further climbing. I only climbed two of the ten. When I jumped for that perfect shot and slipped, it would lead to twenty years of piercing chronic back pain.

while attempting to travel, not to mention a four-hour stay in a 747 disconnected from airport facilities, without water or bathroom necessaries, in 125-degree heat in Pakistan, and facing "don't get out" rifle barrels. I could only see a full load of overheated, desperate passengers and one adventurous colleague. Fortunately, I could also watch one elegant raptor dance in the sky.

Chapter 5, "Can or Can't Be," collects some of my reactions to what I could not justify, accept, comprehend, or do. Sometimes when lost for words or when words were useless, poetry would be the only outlet for my feelings. My travels throughout the United States, Canada, Central America, Netherland Antilles, Belize, Chile, India, Pakistan (short stay), and Korea influenced some of my writings about human issues. And in both "Life's Observable Times" and "Euphoric," they also influenced my sense of splendor.

Chapter 6, "Music, Fiction, and Wrappings," represents the extent to which music and other sounds stimulate me to write. Poetry written to music can take on any form—sad, mellow, or upbeat. My mind, perhaps brainstem, releases a flood of sensations. Sounds of words blend into the music as do different orchestra sections in a concert. When writing to music, my pen moves quickly to keep up with the rhythm. As the music keeps its pace, the words generally pour out of my head. Words are emitted too quickly to be written, let alone intellectualized. Worse, in a way, my pen rarely keeps up with the speed of passing stanzas. An immeasurable quantity of starts trip over themselves. Those mess-ups are mostly scratched out and I start over. A few I have filled in later, without music.

"Music, Fiction, and Wrappings" reflects my responses to people and sometimes my imagination about people—these are fictitious, mostly. The poetry is parallel to an actor's script, where the scriptwriter is me, the script is poetry, and the actor is myself reading or feeling what I've written. These poems are without predestined topics.

Ballet would have considerable influence on my attachments to the arts. I was fortunate that while quite young, I was chosen to perform in the annual Tchaikovsky ballet, *The Nutcracker*, as well being selected to dance with the company dancers in two operas, *La Sonámbula* and *Lohengrin*, in both San Francisco and Los Angeles. During one of those performances in Los Angeles, I made an unforgivable performance error. No, I never progressed to ballerina.

I have no regrets. However, the moment of error was a precious one, both beautiful and humorous, retrospectively[3].

Chapter 7, "Beasts and Child's Play," is definitely imaginary. It consists of silly poems, such as those I wrote during pernicious moments when starving mosquitoes would settle on my skin and extract blood. Beasts and Child's Play is what it seems to be, a collection of poems that exudes, humor, frustrations and strange moods.

Chapter 8, "Ephemeral Streams and Pits," is the bottom of the barrel. Despite the cleaning, if you wish to become depressed, this chapter serves as a sampler. When the centuries turned, my self-esteem was so low, and I was so exhausted, that there wasn't much to hold on to. Even poetry was slipping. My husband, who barely knew me and what he was getting into, kept me treading water. I decided to go forward with brain surgery, removing part of my left temporal lobe[4]. While making decisions and taking neurological tests, I wrote more and more, while experiencing odd sedatives and morphine.

"Ephemeral Streams and Pits" consists of poems that relate my states of mind while at my worst emotionally. Seeing the worst of me, retrospectively, in many of those poems, I chose to edit a few and trash a bunch. Some beauty, inspiration, commitment, and art do exist in the chapter. All of my painful experiences helped me describe and feel at least an element of the pain I encountered in others. Without any of my major setbacks, I wouldn't have been so motivated to share my poetry with you.

Chapter 9, "Euphoric," includes poetry describing what I have felt while visiting and working for parks and biosphere reserves. I specifically dedicate this chapter to the people who establish and maintain natural and historic lands. The out-of-doors stimulates me to write every time I step outside and

---

3   While coming on stage on cue, opening night, I stopped short just as I appeared. The beauty of the music and opera singers' chorus lines were located in the back of the stage. Their voices first shocked and absorbed me. I turned around to face them, all in a minute or less. I stared and my jaw dropped with awe. Of course, I wasn't dancing as instructed, and worse, my back faced the expectant audience for timeless moments. The adult lead dancer dancingly swayed towards me and escorted me, skipping, toward our dancing circle on center stage, facing the audience. The pointed, shark-toothed smiles directed at me on stage told me, "Your days are numbered, kid." On leaving the stage, I learned all of life's vocabulary that would serve me colorfully in sports, frustration bouts, anger, and scholarly arguments. In retrospect, this was a great experience. I've never lost my appreciation of opera and dance, and my feet can't hold still during a good ballet, it's true.

4   Apparently, all my life my left temporal lobe activity was drawn from the right temporal lobe, explaining much of my orientations and approaches in research and planning. In the late 90's I was quite physically ill from work problems, my technical papers really came closer to my approach towards integrating knowledge from entirely different orientations, sciences, applications, culture, and arts. Interestingly, that paper shows there's something wrong with English and format, but it is my favorite. Ironically, it's been a failure.

see what's around me. My friends led me to my adventures with wildlife and parks conservation, beginning with the effort to establish Redwoods National Park back in the late 1960s. You will notice both in Chapter 1 as well as here that my writing about animals and nature are sinfully anthropomorphic[5]. This was derived from several sources. Once in the United States, my family's love of animals became exceptional—thanks to my mom. Her work at the California Academy of Sciences in mammalogy, feeding animals and helping maintain collections and files, had a dull title. Being a "do it all," though, was everything but dull. Besides the usual specimen preparation and collections management, she fed fish and vitamins to fish-eating bats, fetched and cleaned beached marine mammal carcasses, counted sea otters, and helped identify deadly mushrooms for the police department by examining the stomach contents of dead gourmands who made mistakes[6].

Now, thirty years later, not much has changed. Perhaps it's a little less exotic with our cats, dogs, goats, and horses amidst our local Sierra Nevada foothills wildlife.

"Euphoric" comes from the vastness of space, land, and water, and what these all contain. The poems come from times when I've felt inspired and generally optimistic, trusting, and energetic. The feelings of smallness, insignificance, and randomness make me feel secure, strong, and fortunate, even when I am holding on by a string.

Chapter 10, "Religious and Philosophical," is the outpouring of verses that come inevitably when I listen to organ concerts, Bach symphonies, Gregorian chants, Southern gospel music, or the blues, and whenever I tour cathedrals, cemeteries and some ancient monuments. Some poetry results from my preparations for surgery, while relaxed and sedated. Also, on a few of my visits to the Presidio in San Francisco, I've stood at the countless gravestones. There lay the markers of lives that gave me the opportunity to experience freedom. Those lives hold my inspired love and lasting respect. I wrote a few poems there, and left them anonymously outside the chapel door in the early 1990s.

I think that I began putting prayer-verses to music early on in my head. I remember my childhood exposures to Latin chants and Danish services.

---

5   "Anthropomorphic" implies a description of animal behavior imposing humanized inter-pretations of motive and emotion in the description or analysis.

6   She also brought home many of our pets and fostered wildlife. I was her enthusiastic "asso-ciate" in everything from hand feeding bats, fetching beached marine mammals, to caring all the interesting animals that she or I brought home. Our *fauna exotica* included skunks, opossums, slow loris, bushbabies, bats, and parrots. We added the pigeons, fish, tarantulas, scorpions, fence lizards, and naturally cats. (My dad drew the limit with my additions say-ing, "I refuse to come home unless you remove the ##&#$% scorpions from the house!") Our house wasn't that large.

Understanding neither language, I just filled stanzas with my own words, or made what seemed to be the right linguistic sounds. Then I imagined freely what was being sung.

Sometimes, as I grew older, my heart needed to pray to what I always felt was undefined. When away from my mountains or ocean, I would write to open my eyes and "walk" outside of my shell. If God is perfect and limitless, God doesn't need definition, instruction, enforcers, know-it-alls, or clubs. Hell and heaven, being part of the All we experience, provide us with subjects for our inspiration and imagination: music, songs, lives, and poetry.

Sliding back down to earth—Chapter 11, "Slimy Tongue Twister," contains only one story/verse. It is primarily written for a fun time, in any state of learning, euphoria, inebriation, humor, or aging. "Night's Slime Story Tale" is upbeat. It is ironically one true representative of the semi-independent values of words, sounds, rhythm, and meaning. Unequivocally, the master of this was Lewis Carroll, in "Jabberwocky" (1871). Make no mistake— "Night's-Slime Story Tale" is definitely not deep, nor does it compete with Carroll. This story's sound popped into my head out of nowhere and grew. I wrote "Night's Slime Story Tale" to note that spotted, not just striped, skunks exist. Only a crazy biologist would do that. While playing with this story, I quickly realized that I was focused on sounds and speech and neglecting rhyme and meaning.

I wrote "Night's Slime Story Tale" for anyone age ranging from minus nine months to one hundred plus years old[7]. I dare you (or someone) to recite or even read the story out loud clearly, after a classic Friday-after-work evening with friends, a high-sugar-content birthday party full of kids, an elevated wedding reception, or a traditional New Year's celebration. I also suggest you try it in a grammar school or junior high school class. It's a fun tool for learning about language structure, reading, syntax, grammatical errors, spelling, enunciation, rhythms, and word meanings. Kids will laugh; they will even smile if given prizes.

Why publish *One Stranger's Songs*?   Well, when registering for the past two annual San Francisco Writers Conferences, I decided to submit a few poems to their associated poetry competition. This was literally for fun; I didn't plan on hearing anything about the poems. I attended the conference seeking an agent or publisher for my fearsome nonfiction book about gastropods. Both years, I won poetry awards, while drawing a zero with my efforts to publish about gastropods.

---

7   I'm presently preparing this little story for schools as a game for training in reading and vocabulary along with a CD, dictionary, etc.

The poetry awards surprised me, and after receiving some encouragement ("Why don't you share it all?"), I decided to assemble the masses of papers and journals resting under the house in storage boxes full of squirrel winter-stashed acorns and shredded book pages for mouse nests, together with gifts of mouse urine and droppings. It is there where I exhumed most of this poetry. I do have one regret regarding *One Stranger's Songs*. My French, mostly "Franglais" poetry that was part of this original set will be for later[8].

So, *One Stranger's Songs* comprises forty-plus years of responses to people, curses, benedictions, events, explorations, and discoveries up to midway through 2008 for a fifty-eight-and-a-half-year-old idealist, immigrant, scientist, wife, mom, quasi-computer geek, horse/goat/dog/cat/garden keeper, and "manure shoveler"—good exercise.

I love and thank you, Lou. Thank you, Dominique; your life continues to feed my motivations. <<Merci, Maman, Mamine (Gabriel Nuyttens, grandmother), et Papa (Hans Schonewald, father)>> for your examples, stories and both historical and philosophical insights. Thank you, my dear friend Margaret Brown (Minkwitz) for your friendship that stretches back to the late 1950s. You lovingly jabbed me a few months ago to finish this project so that I can start finishing my other many projects and quit complaining. (I'm smiling, Meg!) Thank you, Elizabeth Long (Betsy), my friend and a journalist, for your encouragement, plus your looking over and cleaning up my prose. I would like to thank the countless people who've influenced, encouraged, and inspired my poetry over these forty-plus years.

Also, thank you Kenneth H. Putnam for kindly reading these poems. Your wife was there at the right time and the right place, and was familiar with a perfect poetry lover, namely you. Our conversation in the old historic Coloma post office sent my pages out for your reading. I wanted feedback from someone who knew nothing about me, professionally or otherwise. You generously provided your time, insight, and practical advice regarding what others might see and hear sounding in the collection of *One Stranger's Songs*.

Christine Schonewald
Coloma, California

November 4, 2008

---

8   The French and Franglais poems are some of my earliest.

Contents

Life's Observable Time

THANK LOVE

Here is a thank you
We send with it
Warmth and esteem
Call when you can
Come by
Our house is open
For you
Let us know
When you're near our door
Approach and we'll smile
We'll feel great
And you'll be greeted
Met by hearts
Both tender and warm

WARM AFFECTION

Warm
      Affection
Knowing smile
Soft
      Voice
Embrace
      Want
Strong arms
Grooming
      Hands
Embrace
      Love
Seek affection
Causes
      Stir
Embracing
      Pleasure
Lasting hope
Grounded
      Time

FLOUNDERS AND FLEMISH GUILDS

Flounders and Flemish painters
We tried to pay with Flounders instead of dollars
Only to find our merchant bewildered
Wanting; guilders instead of flounders
We being flustered
Removed our thoughts from flounders
And Flemish painters
And forthwith provided them
With Aruban gilders, rather than dinner

ONE NIGHT

Of one simple night spent in India's splendor
Quiet remembrances stir at dawn's wakening
Like dew drops, silver hangs beautiful reflections
When moisture of my tears and touched emotion
Make my fondness flower
Blossom

GAMBLER IN PARIS

Seine mane
Same man
Sane man
      What do you report?
Lost catch
Loss cash
Loss cashed
      Disappearing ink
Live learn
Life line
Life loan
      Conciliatory act
One's due
One flew
Mirror's view
One escape from
Carry out
      All bearing down
      All being sewn
      On bearing down
      Carry out & so on ...

Shake, Flake, Scrape

Shake dust off me
  Off my exterior
  Superior feeling

Flake bark off me
  Off my interior
  Superior feeling

Scrape dirt off me
  Off my underside
  Superior feeling

Would I wash what's left?
  Cleft face
  Intentions divided

Whitened-white wash
  And deleted feelings

WALKING IN RAIN

Serene dabbles
Mountain climb
When rain lifts me
My legs walk
Switchbacks
Scramble
In placed moments
Lightning
Kindling twigs
Fire's warmth
Grows easily
The red fed
Hot rocks
Then sent orange
Yellow flames, detached
From sources that
Reads (readies, reaches) me
Leaning against fleece
Soft blanket, wearing down
Roasting
On warm seasoned rock

Insomnia Slept

Before a warmth's color
Of one room in couched fleece
Zeke yawns with a sudden
Headshake rattles a collar
While in tandem Monty
Pillow-flaps black ears and
Orients to rest holding
His chin with support
Of white 1-waved fur

Dark rough levity
Scene serine, lip of
Zeke's white muzzle
Tucked on my other side
Melted in white
Brown-camouflaged feathers
Moon-shaped red lids
Raised irises' circles

Wakened ambers
Stove's dry logs

Comfort, breathing slowly
Contrasts
With deep churns
Of Monty's rhythmic waves
Paw a dream's motion

There I sit and relish
A moment, couched
Pillows rest my back
My terry cloth robe
Tucked and warm
Tossed lightly by the
REM sleep on my side

Slowed, I nod off
In hypnosis
Rest's sleep guides me
Eyes shut, feet tracking
Trail to warm covers

What seems soft?

My bed and my fondest
Love, You
Husband sound asleep
Deeply rests, still
From floating ribbons
New light, and
Warmed air streams

We greet morning
Our dreams settling
With distanced stars
Risen mist
Lifts tracings
Of warmed fantasies

ORION

Orion one clear night
City streets absent, no traffic to fight
Milky Way clusters
Seven sisters stay the night
Shooting stars carry souls
Darkness and light
Years develop
Promises unveil

FLINGING LIGHT BULBS

Two orange floats
Three blue boats
One catamaran
One frigate
One bulb
All their litter
Falls when
Non-thought
Makes their sewer

BRIGHT A.M.

Good day, bright day
What is in store for us today?
What is the climate that I feel?
Oh how I wish the cool mountain breeze
Would caress my leather cheeks
That the cold lake waters
Cleanse my soul
To hear perfect silence
But a moment's rest

D.C., AT HOME

A white cat passed by me
Swinging its black tail
The footsteps move toward me
And I hear the motor's rail
Lights pass through bushes
Each in opposite row
The beep, the song,
Hums, and caws of crows
Along white pillars

Raindrops on me
Wet my hair
What is a night that's serene?
This one, after its rain
After its wind, on the river
Even while mosquitoes bite
Dowse my legs with red spots
I'll see the following day

I feel like a queen,
Soft, stoic, serene—feeling
Affections from cleansed air
Whispered songs for my ears
In tandem with and contrast to
All tossed puzzled glances
From gate guards nodding
Wondering while standing
What state this tourist's in
So late, strolling in starlight

DRAWING UP PLANS

A conversation moves
Its shape is split
By the thunder
Wave of the hand
Separated form
Sound and touch seared
I could only see lips move

Cacophonous pantomimes
Stretched far
Across a lobby
Saliva sprayed
Cries rose high
Backs turned
Flouting, "Sorry"
Snubbed
Then "Good-bye"

FRIENDS' GIFTS OF STARS TO SHINE

Good night my friends
Your gift was joyous and tender
You touch and care
Warmed my heart

Your grace and kindness
Gave splendid moments
Shared a lasting dream
You warmed my heart
Brought stars to shine
Pierced a closet's night
Causing the clouds to break
Killed a grey oppression

Your splendid moments
Brought dawn's songs
Whereupon
Light's morning swept in
"Accept my thanks," I said
"I wish you share my joy."

One warm and splendid night
When you sleep softly, enter
Sight and place those
Lasting dreams, where we'll
Meet with all same reference
Sharing light- and age-
Entertaining, all uplifting
Kinds of best memories
That last

Sounds Acting and Timing

Commemorate
      nuff
      sicks
Exonerate
      duff
      licks
Enumerate
      muff
      cricks
Simulate
      snuff
      pricks
Expounding
      picks
      guff
Exuding
      nicks
      stuff
Exacerbating
      kicks
      huff
Exploding
      wicks
      fluff

At one time
At fixed times
Between times
Frequent times
Intermittent times
Never
Single time
Few times
Some times
Many times
Always

TONIC AND LIME

Tonic and lime
Cliff-hanger without the cliff
Rum—sublime
Non-alcoholic stiff
What would it be?
If I had them all
Garbled mind
And painless wonder
Love my dark rum
Quinine tonic, slice of lime

Shattered glass
Spilled lime
Running tonic
Sublime
A wind blew strongly
Shattered glass
Suddenly broken
Spread over
The counter's tile
I had to smile and ask for
More!

SWEET MEMORY

Was it yesterday that we walked in the sun?
Drove in the heat?
Sat in the shade?
I lay beneath the stars
      In admiration of a sky
      So pure
      So serene
Folding my limbs
      For fetal security
Absorbing the warmth
      Of your infinite skies
Capturing each breath and
      Silent contemplation
Where are you now?
My soul is in motion
Where are you now?
      Now far away
Far away from here

CITY POOL SPLASHES

Splashing
Simultaneous voices
Bronzed bodies
White smiles
Brown eyes
Cheerful cries as
      Down under jumping
In warm pool water
Threatening more
      Enjoyment
Carefree smiles
Freedom dives
Childhood races
And twisting leaps
As falling into water
Elated joy

DOCKING A BOAT

Laughter forced through a nostrilled roar
As belly reposes on the man's rested oars
Mustache twitching
As lips vibrate
Speech unending
Others hesitate
Cacophonous microphone
In tropical weather
Wind past my ears
I hear waves thunder
Without the shell
Passed the grunted roar
Passed the mustache twitching
And the rested oars

GIFTED SONGS

Gifted songs
Send melody
In kiss and surrendered
Touch shared union
March moments that
Brought them together

AND AS I MOVE

And as I move
With the wind
You are beyond the moment's edge
I saw you looking here
You asked me with eyes beckoning
Will you love me?
Sweetest heart
A passionate smile
Share our souls
Share our warmth
Let me give you
You gave me
Joint majesty's adoration
In moment's breath
Most lavender moments
Heavenly sonnets

HANDSOME MAN

I met a handsome man tonight
Of course he's far away
Felt a spark; he felt it too
We said "Good-bye"
"Glad to meet you."

DRAGS HIS BROOM

The man in orange drags his broom
From garage gate to large lots
Infinite rows
Carries a white bag
Picks up trash
As the tractor rolls
Picks the trash dumps up
Truck with a sash
Carries the man in orange
With the broom

WORKS WITH WOLVES

Who works with wolves?
I've met several now
All sometime live in the wild
They are closer to the song

In my dreams far outside
I'm a woman on soft humus tundra
(Well, behind the desk—much of the time)
Days' dreams tune on
Songs sung by moonlight
Traveled waves distance
On pure tones
Comforts and renewal
I sing in the nights carousing

Last Night Your Message

Last night your message reached me
Under an ebony sky with powder made of the galaxy's arms
Milky Way claimed an arch connecting opposite horizons
The red iron canyon
So still the sound, only of breezes
Connecting my thoughts to dreams
And their wishes
There I pondered first want
And later deserve
And now simply watch

Poetic beauty
Out of doors
Language use
Seek to share
Demand no secrets
That love and devotion
To whatever is evident
Is mutually blessed

Myriad of Constellations

It's a myriad of constellations
Of efforts and wages
Synchronized dances
Speaking in time
Frolicking dragonflies
Lake-top reflections
Of our satin moon
I feel silk drawn
From cocoons unraided
Incense burns strong
Walloping flight
Fluffed fresh feathers
And bread from heaven
Dangling onlookers set
Red orchids' blossoms
Dressing generations
Earthen young
Raved hordes
Swept doorsteps

MEMORIES OF HOME

Can they merge under a three-quarter moon?
The night walks and poetry and fondest memory
Can they become one as if they'll always replay
My mystical days
So far away now and gone
Alone, caught in memories
Gone grey

YOU'RE THERE

Once on a dark night's river
On land
Just tens of miles from
Home
A crowded room
Watching
Where
You and I were shown a love
That would blossom to last our lives
With few scars
With patches sewn from the past
Uneroded, fed by touching kindness
Hoping, rewarding, soothing
For love to say its mind
Now thanking
Not just in distant poetry

Warmed from the Chill

Moist chill of northern street
Drifted snow slides on ice's shadow
Reflected season in temper's moments
Your arms warm me by inches
By body's whole

THREE—3

Three is a varied number of multiple meanings
Three theorems can be drawn and from these
3 infinitum descriptions met
Three can be superstitious
Three can be counting
And three can describe
Three or multiples of three things
  describe a dimension
  describe religion
  describe social tension
And in the latter there are three things
  The first is unwillingness
  The second is unevenness
  The third is competitiveness
Their multiple is the harm

NEAR BANGALORE

It doesn't take much to remember
      All these feelings
Warm and solicitous around a small
      Fir tree
When alone you took us in your care
      And
Wished us "peace on earth"
We wished you
—"goodwill toward men"

You sang for us and fed us when
      We longed for
Our loved ones at home singing us
      Lullabies
Thank you good people for your
      Friendship
What all people should be to
      Each other
Whenever, then, and
      Remain
God bless you all, each in your
      Way
Merry wishes, health
      Happiness
Christmas Day!

SUN SPOKE AT 7:30

Today the sun spoke at 7:30
I was ready
Having listened to its voice as it was yawning
Awakening

The mornings for each creature stir
And never would I wish
To be left back alone
Without them

Anticipations haven't reached yet
Arms extend over the chasm
Drafts swell and weaken
The resolve to hold them
Toward me
And we wish it could have been

Forest Walk

Light flows between your fingers
Reflecting all mirrors of color
Broadening fantastic dreams
Guiding attentive spirits' curiosities
Nourishing them all with silk
Homespun and vases carved
Forest sandalwood, tropical hardwood
Decor of nacre inlays
Cause us to reflect, arrive partway

Love's Note

I had to write just one more to say
What a good feeling I have right now
You must be doing well
And your thoughts must be at peace
Remember this moment
If you see me again
And let me know I reached you
With great affection

An Earlier Time

Blank page
I'll wage
You leave our hearts blank-slated

On stage
We'll wage
Past times will arch unnoticed

Why page?
Won't gauge?
Why love's loss was predicted?

Be sage
Let's wage
Spent love's emaciated

(I'll rephrase)

Good night
Sweet knight
Come some next-time, created

Vacation's Relaxation

He exits the room
Onto the deck
Looks out
After resting
Cannot relax
He strains
To lie back
In his chair
He's pensive
Thoughts convulsive
On reflection regains
Passing, momentary feeling
Of where he's been
He's gone now

Deck chair is vacant
Its blue, white pattern alone
Cloth, it's dark now
Through the dim pane window

Shadows leave
The empty room
He comes back
They're two now

He's sulking, standing
He's lost now I see
He's wishing but
Vacation is ending
Before he'd felt it
They would leave

A Source without Definition

The essence of what I know
Leads me searching, drawn
Hopes once fulfilled
Wished perception
Humanly understand
With all ups and downs

Do you shine?
A beauty, intricate and whole?
Attributes, your treasures, frame
Happier moments, expansive
Flux spreads your shine
Casts a radiance, formed
Impermeable
Demolished crises seem
Deliberate targets, power
Hovers, transcendent
Skies vast, thin, humans pull
It seems, left unsupported
Undirected, weighted, elements
Massed constant motion
Surrounding, piercing collisions

Would you shine?
Bodies and lives tossed
Can some find order
Invulnerable rest,
Motion chosen as direct
Rendered to humanity?
Or wishes, hopes orchestrate?
Can pleas have attraction,
Answers' projections,
Innocently founded solutions?

Or all lie unnoticed, untoward
Not away, nor still
Unencountered
Coldly impartial and diffuse?

Enviable Canid Sleep

Thin skin from the
      Hairline
Warm and soft
      In expression
Shaded black and
      Glossed nose tip
Pink inside
      Not red like the flesh gum line
Frisked heart beat
Eyes steam affection
Brown hair
      Impressing
Of the pup's
      Warm nasal breath
Where all in social
      Graces hover staring
      Scents curl and cuddle
On the old couch
Without fuss

Resort's Deck

Parasols escalated elevated
    Serrated edge decor
Dexterous folded chairs with
    Table settings proxy home
Rental serene resort in
    Rafted forests planted
As lumps reform, melted
    In weight gained lost
A wakened adrenaline
    Provides scenic weight tosses
In coral headways and
    Clean surrounds and vision
Whitened losses, death's lost color
    Seen as imprint of sand
Clouds cover deepening triggers
    Of extracted and consumptive pleasure

A BEGINNING

The afterward of a bird's song
Alights my leaded feet
Trodden paths and mule dung
Keep the scarab on its beat
Twice again a spider weaves
His silken web about me
Entangled, yes I am, I feel
The network of spring demanding

ALTERNATIVES

To seek peace is to seek adventure
Complication, distress
Worried unhappiness, and grief
But these are only alternative rewards
For seeking
Because seeking can bring you
Peace with understanding, love, and life
In crystal novelty and purity
Blemish-able only by your susceptibility to the
Alternatives

PARTING WINGS

Soul nests in parting wings
　　　From the body
Stretch over water ripples
　　　In lake movements
Marsh land's edges and
　　　In pressing moments
I see the solitude in me
　　　Reflected in the water
No, it's not my reflection
　　　But some past way
The glide of still vapors
　　　Of morning's mists
Rising from the warmth
　　　Of lake streams
Into cold air

HOME

Fog rolls
Tumbling over eucalyptus
Bowing to the beauty of the bay
Tumbling gracefully
And dancing in setting sun rays
Reflecting light
It inhales the freshness
Of the first spring morning and
With newly taken breath pours
Forth a warm, salty breeze
Chilled for ecstasy
Beauty is invalid in the eyes of nature
For it is a poor explanation of the
Perfection that we survey
For which we know
No exclamation

Wing the Air

Lift, fog, lift
Your umbrella
So your sheets
Will feel fresh air
Turn your linens to the
Sky so sunshine will
Dry the mildew
Lift your eyes
Lift our engines
Soar, lift your nose
      To small winds
Inner land's sea breeze
Pale and fair
No signature
No statue or
Standing stalemate
Merely standing ease
In your bird's flight

EVOLVING MORE

One gram to one calorie raises one degree
And so the oceans will boil eternity
One cell, two blastulas form—twain
Step, dance quickly, and regress again

One oxygen, two hydrogens, and carbon bond
Then nitrogen, hydrogen, ammonia, codons
One double helix to computer intrigues
Square roots of minus four, 2i succeeds

One life's line drive resounds and transforms
To planar lines and dimensions reform
Sphere's world rests its weight on all four
Leaving its time-space as flatland, a bore

TIME IS LONG

Where are your thoughts?
Where is your soul?
What is the nature of your mood?
I am thinking of you
Wishing you were beside me
For I am alone as I am here

Sinuous time passes
Without rushing, without slowing
Moving constantly as we measure
But of its essence lighten
Time would disappear
If I weren't here to measure

IMPULSE

I will write more
It is in me
My pen of its own will
Governs my hand to motion
My fingers bend and right wrist slides
With the motion of the poem
Or is it yours, whoever you are
Who gives me the power to write?

I'm moving forward
Onward now and not stalling
I feel a twinkling impulse
Lifting or guiding me
I will get there
I will get free

"Advisors"

He sang a sweet song of motionless whispers
The faintness of his accent directed our inspiration
And he left with our silent responses to his pleas
His thirst satisfied but because thirst became foreign
By the cruel dissection of his imagination
Tormented by desires of comprehension
Of a part that he could not reveal
Not knowing himself
And we not knowing him more than himself
Bred strange incongruities in our philosophies
All falsified our better motives, transforming them
We imposed our incongruities on his insecurities
And destroyed the better elements of his introspection

Wandering

Beauty is but a vain and doubtful good
A shining gloss that's suddenly faded
A flower that dies when first it goes to bud
A brittle glass that's broken, presently
A doubtful good, a gloss, a glass, a flower
Lost, faded, broken, dead within the hour

Sun's Silk Sets

Releasing its ribbons
Fresh-woven silks
Floating for inspection
By brown hands
Whisper dreaming colors brightest
Sunset
Like lives unfolding and paradox
Giving way to new paths
While mending
Old roads
Ageless beauty stands
Veiled from superficial inspection
And runs
Out of sight from tourist's fur
Beside herself
Dips into night

ONE TIDE

It's really quite beautiful here on the beach
Young couples teasing, cuddling
Couples, young with small children
Holding each other, kissing, cuddling
Wanting to make love

Countless smiles of understanding exchange
Sifted moments between
Grains of sand
Slip between rumbling waves
On this beach
Continuous motion

Recycling pleasures
Love's redundant pleasures
Spilling forth on the third day of spring
Were we to join them, would we be shy?
Wish you could hold me now
Wish you would kiss me now
Love me and seemingly
Endless afternoon, endless distance
In spring's kind sun
Warm on the beach
Clutching souls and passions
In memory's endless wave

My Soul

It was much like a dream
Where my arms stretched before me
Led the way in my sleep
I felt the floor, walls, and doors
All about me, and yet they weren't there
Or was it that I was away
A departed guest, almost a stranger
But not yet, you (my soul) have taken me back
I can write these now, alive

IN MY MIND A THOUGHT: BELIZE SHORES

There was in my mind a thought just passed by
I don't fully remember what it concerned, my
Only reward for a morning's laziness
Watching fish, my flesh fries, scorched
That's life, in the water as watching fish swim by

Quick like my thoughts in their fleeting moments
Diverse like daydreams, beauteous songs and sonnets
I watched them for hours while years will
Romanticize my times in these tropics
As the best of my thirties, forties, fifties rich,
Wilder and honest
Endless ... good times

SUMMER FAREWELL

Dust
Cars
Cows—chewing their food
Rabbits DOR
And waiting for a condolence from the day
To tell me it's OK
"It's OK." "It'll be OK."
Rest there and be fine
Let your concerns fade on
The light fades in the street
Waiting the awakening
Of the street lamp
Summer
Sweats
My energy drains
With each drop vaporized
Touch me and
You'll find I'm not solid
I miss you from another side
Whatever form you took
Whatever wholeness gave
To you
To my life
Once was here

AWAKENING MONDAY

Wake with me
Soft alarm
The dawn passes
Young stars set sooner
As morning passes
Into light of midday
And coffee's awakening
Motion continuous
Stirring passes

DREAM

For as the lights brighten a shrouded building
Amber webs of night's silk glow and descend

Glimmering worlds—depression abolished
Ethereal feelings and hopes grow refurnished

Lit horizons revive clouded worlds
Rain clears, pensive fogs—all dissipate

A hidden world reappears enlivened
Lit, embracing love's replenished strength

Endless voyage set eternally enterprising
Life's long love—one fresh water falling spring

Red-and-Yellow-Striped Pedigree

Red-and-yellow-striped pedigree
White shirts and black ties converge
Open a gate
"Your orders please!"
Spoken non-English
And soothing breeze
Red-and-yellow-striped pedigree
Oohing the blue-striped ship at sea
Currents greet as they converge
All ceremonious in their surge

REVERSE

Rest in fleeting
Writing my lines
Poets are broke
No way to survive
Giving life
Through fond
Words exclamations
Give me support
Rests revelations
Let the effect
Cause the afterward
Fond recourse
When work over done
Cries: "I need escape!"
Where will this be?

What do artists do?
When insurance dies
Blue cover a spirit
All tensions rise
What do you do?
They remember you

LAZY IN HOT HUMIDITY

I felt so lazy today in this very moist air
So much so that I only felt like sleep
The only action that seemed fair
Good meal, coffee, and a swim in the deep
Offered, "Sea or pool?"
The sea I preferred
But it was night, there was no time
Sleep was deferred
And the sip of ocean water
Sea coral will be
Tomorrow

SLEEPING ON THE ROAD—NEVER BEEN SO ...

Never been so tired
As these last few days driving
The lids on my eyes were sleeping
My thoughts lifted
Not held by gravity's constraints
Feeling gone
From my body, emaciated
The time taking its swing
Across my dreams
Imagined the—real thoughts
Unconscious trained
Places drift—by and through me
Sleep posses me until I awake
To see the steel and asphalt
Puttered road near concrete
At the stop sign
Standing still
Tires screeching

PALMETTO'S PRIME

Palmetto's prime
Palm's dime
Yucca's time

Sea grapes
Hotel drapes
Hotel gates
White sand
Hollow man
Cool fan

Tasty drink
I think
The man winks

At me
By the sea
Holiday spree

QUANDARY—A CROWD STANDING

Quandary
Questions
Use of few words
Seems little
For all worlds
My eyes see
Folly
Frustration
Mind's lips fall short

Empty Sleep

Sleep carefully, sleep sweetly, but open your ears
For dawn's early rustling lays open the fears
Of tomorrow that's coming dangers anew
Surprises of late risers—they're after you!
Smile happily, breathe freely, and show not your tears
For sadness when creeping will plague your years
Remember in bad times those who really care
You are number one and all others finish few
If life becomes lonely to the grave
It surely steers
Keep yourself social, stable, self-secure
And from traps of all loneliness keep clear

YOUR CHAIR IS FOLDED

Your chair is folded
And blown over from wind
Your shutters closed
And you refrain
From moving outside
From exterior seeing
You hide from air's passing
That feeds you
You're living

"Where are you?
        Where do your thoughts lie?"

"They lie
        When they say they're fine."

Good moods are passing
—Ghost smoking
So vent your words and stress
Don't leave me out there
Helpless bound
Exhume your warmth

CANDIED CHERRIES AND CHOICES

Candied cherries
Horrible confection
Cherries, fresh?
Don't give me cherries
Just sugar fresh
On the 5¢ machine

CHRISTMAS SHOPPING

It is nearly Christmas
And I am left to dream
Of what I can give to those I love
Yet wishes of good health and dearest love
Must keep warm
Be of the greatest gifts to them
I will gladly give of what I possess
And that is nothing
How does one make love the greatest gift?

Join Me in the Water

Could one be younger?
Having more fun?
Handsomest surroundings
You, resting on your buns
Wish you were with me
I'd surely have more fun
If that were possible
Under this tropical sun
Do join me, come, step
Down just four-hundred-foot stairs
This special time
Share an ecstasy's sea

Tonight with the stars
With the revelry
Arms of anemone
While restful joys want
Calmness
Now, joy's bright
Lovely
Ephemeron
Paean sung

TWENTY YEARS BETWEEN

It's so non modern
They say
So left behind
Away
In stasis for
Days
      On end

Twenty years later
I've seen
Roads bend
Turn about
India's here
When I dial
They say
"Tech support" ...
"What do you need?"
I politely answer
Whatever
Expounding specifics
Immediate replies
      Ask , "When?"
Where?
Support me
Quash tape
Close deal

Young Pool's Body

Blue strips
White hips
Shoes of leather
Long hair
Don't dare
Men will gather

'Round when
See them
Blue eyes graze her
Bare them
Heads turn
Men hear laughter

TREASURED PRESENT FROM INDIA 12/25

The tree's branches were spiral, half-inch diameter
They were opposite forty-five degrees in angles
Tree's base stem polished with silver foil
Three feet high
Styrofoam chips flakes on the bottom
Of cloud's cotton on the table
Hanging bulbs of small foil rappers
A drawn axis deer with full rack
And Santa, made with care
Topped by a star set
In soft cotton clouds
On the tree's top
And silken branches
Permanent memory

POINT-TO-POINT IN MUSIC

Talent
Outstanding
Young and testing
Unusual
Extraordinary
Talent for painting
Singing
Playing
Painting comes alive
Gone for
Time's span
Generation's young

BE GONE, DO

The media event
When all come together
And fear what forever
But smiles sway hearts
And you wonder what, if ever
We could all talk
One people
If we could talk
One set, with children
Beset with problems
Singular moments
Toward life's next stop
Be gone, do
Dump—draw on
The final breath that's exhaled
This process

MORNING AFTER WATCHING

Hard sell as wrinkles walk by on the street
Painted faces with the tans of yesterday
Holding hands and billfolds

Calm and tenderly on the other side
Sway hips waiting greeting a bouncer (cold)
And summer, really winter, greets the guest

Glad to be here though, my pen watches
Tanned, new-wave dye, an earlobe pierced for the morning

The cook sleeps and morning coffee
Scented with late sleeping
The smile of the kindly face
To simplify what is already soft
Most simple and explicit
A sincere morning golden grace

ANTHROPOGENIC SLIP, OR "DOLCE-DOG"

Soft bellowing, breadths
Strong firm bone-ribbed cove
Inhaling air and
Exhaling sweet love
As fine air sifts from lung
To breathe, exhale

Lone emblem dolce soul
Concentrating love
Kind perception smiles
Dimpled sight
Humor laden with
      A graced love in
        Tender movements
        Garden like beauty
In novel and unlike
Kept love, grows
Willed love—and fed
Generating the
Most rapacious future
Appetite for all
Heart's aperture in the eyes
Toward growth, inevitably
A dog

Does It Make Any Difference?

Does it make any difference?
Does blocking discourse help
Is one-on-one better
Than the group therapy
Of applause of media?
What will matter in the end?
All the protests, discussions
Orations went down with
Neuron's culture
Seeking to see—hear
Hand pats on the microphone
So we can hear

Tastes

The tea came in little white bowls
Without the dragon that the teapot had
Simmering, though, a fragrance of jot jasmine
Fried prawns meander 'round with lazy Susan
The hungry table feeds itself
Mustard and tomato—delightfully spiced
Chow yuk, all appetizing, sends
Harmonious flavors through my mouth

GROUP LAUGHTER

Laughter
Laughing
Laugh well
Long well
Hear well
See well
How well
I will
Laugh well
So well
That, well
I will
Be well
In well
The well
Of youth's water
Laughter

Sun's Red-Backed Yellow Chairs

Yellow chairs, one with body
Lying there
Face down
Arms down
Strap undone
Not brown but burning
Blond hair
White feet
Red back
Aw, painful sleep!

DINNER IN NEW ORLEANS

Walking down the streets
In a carefree, happy fashion
With a warmth in my heart
And a thrill for life
For this moment captured once
At the warm candlelight
The jazz moves the soul
And I wait to fly

EVENING WITHOUT STRANGERS

Goodnight, my friends
Your gift was joyous and tender
You touch and care
Warmed my heart and doused the night
In great splendor

DELICATE TREE

Small stars
Strewn over
Delicate green limbs
Soft-spoken
Messages of season
Solo on a night's eve
Sung to all directions
A verdant lace
Long-term memory

FOOTHILL DRIVE

Cars gliding on down a slope
Purple trees align demarcations
Where one car's engine stops
Young dog steps out
There does his business

This car's stops cease
No end sought
While pleasant, while passing
Masses of flowing red rock
Miles, miles, mph
New White Mountains appear at last

Vast, approach
Snowflakes on a silver fender
Pass by, speeding, tapping on glass
Tapping on glass as hail
Then by solar heats transform

Slow trickles soon dry

Elevations reminisce
Winter's lasting storm

GIFT OF A ROSE

I need you, and my love for you does not die
The thought of a red rose, a warm smile, and your eyes
Casts a shadow on my restlessness
I rest, taking part in pleasant dreams of days
Kind words, caring and unselfish thoughts we've shared
Sing to me, seeming timeless
For still one more moment

MARKERS—VIDEO

Hold and constrain
Trap and store
Restrain
Block interface interference
Block movement or access
Support culturally
Support structurally
Assist and embellish
Attracted attention
Certify location
Shade and restore
Funnel then bridge
Organize and partition
Demonstrate function
Explore

ONLY FOR THE BREEZE

If it were only for the breeze
I'd know not where I was
Were it only the heat
I'd think where I was
Palm trees grow anywhere
Where there's tropical heat
And winter need not freeze
White sand need not be treaded
Under my sensitive feet
Yet smells of the air given
Trade answers in my sleep

Why then do I think
I am anywhere but
In the nearest tropical sink
Where relaxation
Soft incline prevent
Imaginations to escape
The present

AIRPORT'S ORANGE JANITOR

Orange bulb
Not glowing
Not turned on yet
Summer's light
Still strong
The sun's not down yet
Hey man
Free man
You've got no rest
Working man fine hand
You're not done yet

BREATH

Who lies beneath the white ceiling?
Face, crushed in the pillow
      Deeply in slumber
I want your thoughts
I hope for your warmth
I am so thirsty
For your affection
      Loving hands
      A breath from soft whispers
A brow of sweat
As I see our love
As our eyes cling
Two warmed bodies
Our spirits transposed
      Moving across
      Exchanging worlds
Where time dissipates

MUSIC TO SLEEP

Saving time
Dining on sleep
Stanzas repeat themselves
Gone whence they dance themselves
To sleep
A long rest
Won't dream
Arrest life
Sound awake
Seems

Solitaire

To want a poem
To write a feeling
Demand more than want
Knowing if I look
Into myself
Stir my feeling
Maybe I'll grab
All sense before me

Night's Paltry Air—One Night in D.C.

Humid density
Weighs heavily on my lungs
Crickets' rhapsody
Fireflies' madness
Seeming paradise once it has cooled
Dark night, star-bright
Sky with city aura
Denuded aura
Stars are dim
Seem so far
Moon eruptive
Breath
Interrupted
In a humid sink
Of air, water, humid soup
Welcome back
Fall, in water's weight
Left summer's hope
Here squinting
Actually smiling
Tantalized
Caught, stuck
Smiling after all
Humorously

OLD MAN IN THE CAFÉ, TALKING

Ripples of fat hang out of the sweater
The belly hangs over the belt
The soft and pouched cheeks
Are the masques for the sorrows?

Warm inside with a joyful air
Jovial to some who don't see despair
Trying to fit
Trying to love
Wishing for love
To be at bidding

ONE MOMENT

Call me mildly to absorb
Every thought, each emotion
Blend into one, bright aster cluster
Energetic bind and afterglow
I ponder my moment's thought
And tomorrow

PASSION

I love you, my dear
As the mountain top or green garden
As the gurgling stream flowing on granite
As the alpine meadow and red wildflowers
I love you, my good man
      As I do the pounding ocean
      As I do the fog rolling in
      As I do the mist that splashes upon my breasts

RANDOM WALK

Each moves
From a sole room
Single file

Hidden inside
Wheels turn
Takes them
Far again

Round trip
To dinner
To pest
To vendor?

SING, ALL AS ONE

CONDOR WINGS
The windswept mountains of Southern California
The searching flight of the godhead
The expanse of superior wings
And vector force does lift
A mighty condor to the sky
The last one that exists

"Why search you so endlessly, so alone?
       Why set you not on a peak or pinnacle
       Or find your peace at home?"

"I have no home," said the wing span
       (White crowned symbol)
       No ones with whom to share life's wide airspace
       For I am a sonnet's last breath
       In this air."

It's man's desire to be alone
And with negligent destruction
They've gone
Ideals thinned and peeled
All off—we found only
A memory's last solitaire

POLAR WHITE
Glacial snows show green as earth's caps melt
Searching swimmer heaves
Bear's white mass launches
And cracks its glacial rest
Dives, surfaces for lost food
Lost snow holes and shelves

"Why search you so endlessly, so alone?
       Why not rest on the pole's glacial crust?
       Why don't others come to feed?"

"I have no home," said the white bear
    (Global climate symbol)
    No ones with whom to join for birth on glacial space
    I am no mother, but the last polar bear
    My night's groans drown the air."

It's our desire to be alone
And with negligent destruction
Climate's temporal balances gone
Not just for one time; all follows
Left decomposing, once incubatious times
Humanity's—lost incandescent

DRIFTING

I feel right now as I've never felt before
Happy, yes, though even more unsure
Sad, no, but closer yet to the deep aches that occur
Loneliness is farther, as if I had never known it
Clinging to me is a feeling of fulfillment
How it is, though, that my feelings are so strange
In a small world of my own
A world quite unknown

Life proceeds along its path of red carpets
Intermittent rain puddles
Start the freshness of the autumn wind, fall
Leaves cracking under my feet look
Different—as they never had before
It's love? Bent, reckless, cautious
Emotions unveil, at least to the self
The churning of my stomach—just whining
Logic, my intellect precipitates

My emotion is contained and momentarily
I am suspended
Happiness is animating, new, momentous
Perhaps one day I'll be reminiscing.

SONG TO A BATTLE'S GHOST

Clear specter mirrors and casting devotions
Seeming might crumbles in air
Plenty remarks at her loss of invention
And desperately alights in dull detention
    To hide
Let me guide and lift your heart
Let me wrap your sorrow, loneliness
Caught in harping triumph of battle
In ways which differ from your instruction
I'll carry your soul to sky-lit meadows
There sink all fears from fighting war
Trade away tension for simpler colorations
Add honest serenity for sight's open song
    In stride

Starts Nightfall

Light reflects off of my right leg in the dark of the early night
My shoe contrasts due to this light against the green grass blades
My other foot rests on its side, facing the drier tomorrow
Small plants bent underweight point to only to see clouds running
But their roots wake up the pleasure sent to them from skyline
And atmospheres cleansed of sorrow bend their dew to earth's design
Fresh air as I see a red skirt, green mother earth she rests
Sleeping gently

LOOKING THROUGH THE WINDOW

A forceful nature pulls at my worn remains
And lost I am in this midst, I cannot walk or run

Lights on my heavy body that treads in sullen earth
Relieve it of its sadness; give it comfort in your hearth

The bars that separate me from your windowpane
Are thick and cast of iron
Renew the force by which it abides to give it a livened and
animate hue

Oh, dank and dark, a world will die if one let it have its way
And yet, within its inner core, hope flickers there to stay

Away, away those thoughts do fly off from my rancid soul
Away, afar, they soar far removed, off for a while, at least

There the mountain stream recalls where the joy reigns supreme
Oh, hurry! Then my spirit catches the faintness of my dream

To that glacier's tip steadfast it moves where crevice pierces ice
A soul long-lived with its armament in waiting resigns

So quiet it lies there and still a sound is felt
Reverberations on an iced expanse; soft flutters of a glacial bird

It flies swiftly as my soul would do and seeks its rest at home
Which for us is this distant place, curious and happy abode?

Swifter, higher, lower; let me reach! You fly too far for me
My mind in whirling is senseless and leaves its corpse behind for
posterity

TIMELESS THOUGHTS

The moon shifts with the azimuth
Life is carried by the wind
I feel my lover's breath whisper
With cream-like softness in my ear
I see his chest rise and fall
As the ocean tides ebb and flow
As each sea creature takes in water
Life-giving fluid and holds it all, exposed
Exposed and vulnerable he is
And with deep breaths, dreams
Of his life's loves and fantasies
Of his years yet unlived
As vulnerable as an anchor
Just pierced through spring soil
Or exposing anemone
Tides recede
My eyes like air dwell
All about him
I love him when he sleeps so
With peace and calm dreams
It makes one want to enter
In his closest harbored soul
I'd join him in his wanderings
Through fantasies he holds
To breathtaking adventures
Thriving upon
A spring courtship
He woos me
An atmosphere in waves
Air dancing, bowing, bending, loping around me
Like the handsomest crane
It presents him
In desperate love's adventure
To mate again
I love him
Comfort we've found in our dream
At peace in partnered life

In duet we move about the
Rows, columns, and avenues
Foothills and lost towns
Draw our lives, blood and calms
Scenes of our touching
And as he dreams
I've entered weightless
Joining

LAY HERE ALONE

As I lay here alone
I can't help but let wander
My mind as it roams
To times of first joys
Innocent stutters

I dreamt of times last night
When we were two decades gone
How I left all in cold flight
Without sensing thought

Dream's sleep woke rather early
Its pageant stopped
Its rest abruptly cut off center
Leaving abandoned naiveté
Dawned a crisp morning
Frosted losing sensitivity

I see decades in my dreams
Where we have forgiven all harm
Forgotten inconsequential pains
And there it all seems
Life renewed its fresh start
Each time

TUNES TO A COPPERSMITH'S HAMMER

Now darkness waits to rest
As light lifts itself
I feel light, woken by
A hum of crickets, frogs
Nightly songs of foxes
Breezes gently sweep
Toss my hair feeling
Silken in the night

From the rain that fell
All seven senses say, "It's lovely"
Feeling a dignity
Day's transition to night
As all celebrate
The grouse, an owl, raven's echo
Each sings tonight

I heard them with the coppersmith
At end of rain when drizzle fell
Still, night does set itself
Ever gently down
On its cycle, waiting
For tomorrow's day
And ever will

PLACER VILLA'S BELL

The bell was silent
Its hidden demeanor
Countless interests
Center chronologies
In one wardrobe lay
Underdressed ribbons
Circumscribe one
Timeless treasure
Resounding song
Wagon trains come

COLD

Glistening fossils in a writer's hand
Selling foundations for prior times
Seeing drawn graces painted up right
Beaming headlights unlock sunlight

New Year

At this time between two celebrations
Festive dinners and reminiscing of a past year
Well into a new decade with news unforeseen
Of changing events in time
Charity and happiness in eyes of crowds
Give light to hope
That New Years following will
Fulfill them
Richness of human kindness exposing
The values of friendship
I am indebted to those
Who have brought this joy to me

STROLLING

Arbor
Made from mahogany
Large trunks
Bent over roads
Lights
Dashing
Cars move fast
As bird drops fall on me
Walk
Night
Alone
Out of sight
When footsteps approach me
From behind
Noise comes
Cross walk
Voice translucent
Transparent
Footsteps echo past me
Cross the dotted line
Revved engine
Remember
The familiar smiles
Of roosts that could be
Home
Sensuous night
Longing
No miles
Not disparate
Not sinking despite me
Tasting
Quiet sounds
Night's sounds
Calm breath's canopy

Rock at the Graveyard

Given moment to sing and sew
Let her hair flow
Given life and love's ring, shows
He loved her wearing
  Gold clothes
Whitened hands, washed rock
Pale, solvent hands
Weary both deck
Seeing letters bound
On graved rocks
Cemetery charters
Death defy
As both met souls touched
From two loves
Kiss, he on his knees
Kissing ground stone
Out of body she
Named hums her sound
Fond report missed may
Lovers touch
Can be death's sorrow
Then suck away all darkness
Eject sorrow's chain
Hell's disorder lost
Insignificant hunger

FIRST BLOOM

A columbine sways
In the faintest breeze
Sweet smell of streams
And shadows, green hills
Rocks where they lay
And ice as it gently melts
Into soft green
White lilies
Laden with dew
Belong to the early frost
Of spring's first morning
I hear your chant
The bubbling echo
Of granite jetties
In small glacial creeks
Those sing to my ears

Soft Feline

Eye's deceits and distortion
Blind impermanence
Fetal fat
Love's cat
Docile for petting
Lovely caring
Simulating all
Devoted loved one
For food
This cat and that

OUTSIDE

Ropes of hair
Hanging braided
Youth's hand
Pointing up
Ready for the window
Or skylight
Reaching
Life's window

ALPS CHALET

As the old chin drops its hairs
She sees a face, though it's hidden
Glimmer of his eyes, black diamonds
See the wealth his bushy brows
Her neck's still hers—
A secret turned present with love's kiss
She shares with him
Tenderly they share this winter's night
Toasting four feet on the fireplace
Beginning their dreams for the night

FRESH AFFECTION'S SCENTS

Getting along and bitter weather
Strained loving and battered friendship
Complaint weds generation's learning
Far from fresh scents to follow
We yearn for affection
Feeling only rejection

A Dull Mind's White Ink

I sat today
In the bright white office
Looking at what future
Did not hold for me
Sipping tea I thought,
In the filtered light shade
Why am I not brighter?
The talent I see before me
Only makes me grieve
Where if I hadn't sought out
I'd feel bliss of winter's eve
Naive and innocent thought

MY ACOUCHI DIED[9]

I'll never forget
My little acouchi
She filled curiosity
Fed joy
She was alive
I fed her
Cared and cleaned
But my ignorance
Laziness?
Let her die
I'll not forget
The milk turned
Eastern heat
Summer and I
We choked her life

---

9   My acouchi really belonged to the National Zoological Park in Washington, D.C. It had just been born but was abandoned by her mother. So I stepped in to raise her and accidentally killed her. The acouchi's Latin name is *Myoprocta pratti*. Native to South American tropical forests, acouchis are rodents related to squirrels, mice, gophers, and such. Acouchis look like miniature deer, standing nearly one foot high with slender and graceful legs, and a short deer-like tail. They're also colored like our forest deer or small African duikers. Instead of eating grass, leaves, and twigs, acouchis are fruit eaters with big rodent front teeth.

COMFORT

Seeing snow-crested miracles that lay before me
Nature's expression

As it created me
Insignificant

Life's miniscule operations overbear
Yet I breathe air

An inspiration
Independently lasts

Each moment drifts
To no proper place

While at the corner
Awakened, absorbed

My heart beating gently
And thoughts breathe timelessly

A Time's Contrast: Cast in Bronze

Smooth skin
Water melts
Over skeletal grace
As he works
In damp weather

Brightened
Light's reflection
Skin shining
Hair's gloss
Combed luxurious
Handsome mind
He points a way
To call, to pray
Work and pay

Clearly pale
Bronze cast
Sets a tension
Of motion
Freedom
Cry money
Claim beauty

Blossomed culture
Ingests weight
Shapes retrieve
A past
Resolved and lost
Disposed lightly
So quickly
We pay, in memory

MELANCHOLIC PASSION

Banalities have left me and thoughts are once again creative
Feelings of emptiness have flown and full, rich water flows
    From bubbling streams
    Pouring over granite
Rocks in the purest spring mornings
My soul is happy and my heart sings out
To the new morning, greeting enthusiasms
Molds it in a most natural way

THE SQUID AFTER THE BAR STOP

Sunday daiquiri
Under palm-swayed shade
Sun making its way down
To tropical sea's horizon
Northern sunset
Cloud-studded sky
Carries the frigate bird
And pelican's hunt

Features bring back
My dreams to reefs
Of a tropical sky

I breech the waves
And surface layer
Warmed, blue, clean water
Caribbean origin
Island's splendor
Kinship
Of fine coral sands

Reach out
Bright anemone arms
Green eyes
Matching green kelp
Floating
Amid sea fan clusters
Breathless
Weightless
Absorbing beauty

GOODNIGHT, MY DAUGHTER

Goodnight, my daughter
    Dream calmly tonight
Of friendly times and traditions
    Of mine and Father's love
As we dream of you
    And the joy you have brought us
As we think of you
    Of the wholeness you bring
Your laughter, your sighs
    Your imitations and gestures
Bless our lives
    With thoughts of tomorrow
You are the babe, only eight pounds
    And ounces
Our hands, arms, now our shoulders
    We give as your cradle
Fond dreams and realities
    Be yours for your lifetime
Fond dreams and realities
    Look to tomorrow

DANCER

Their art was beautiful
Though little remains
They were elegant and sailed through the air
Such beauty was everlasting
So it should have been

LOST IN NIGHT

Raptor singer
Predator earth
Sundance brighten
Song of the earth
Given summit,
Foreign displeasure
Confines lost and
Time lost measure

Bird Songs in India

It will likely be years
Before we cross paths again
India changed, incomers, too
I wish you all the best

There's been few more deserving
I've lost my hosts, new friends
I've lost my teacher for evening walks
On birds, mammals, religion, and culture
It's empty here without your flora

Birds' songs search for a morning ear
I could see beauty's sari cross the city
And now it's hard, ten hours away
The simplest gifts surpass
A thirty-great-day residence

You've become a good memory, friend
In so short a time, I've come to see
Learn, I hope well

Caught in my hosts' hearts with each line
Like chants, the colors mesmerize
The subjects come alive in my hands
And with more than just fondness, recollect
What a kindred spirits I found in India
Six thousand miles from all points of reference
So unlikely, and one of too few

Your forests, riparian lands
Release all emotions, ethereal, you know
Truly inspired as prayers, as poems

STRATIFIED SKY

Opera thunders and stratified sky
Omnivorous clashes and cacophonous cry
Streaked light swept across
The sky as if spreading
Down ravines and throng gullies pry
The water walls on land
Flood your homes and crops
Wasting wet and they die
From silt swept
Monsoon weather

Ravenous clacks under mud and flood lay

There's light on the horizon
Just above the tree line, flat here
Like a ribbon of greenish grey
Taught on the skyline
Where air meets land and mudded grasses
Exchange and water drips
Downward to soil absorption
And runoff stains into river's swells
The ravenous appetite

WOVEN SYMBOLS - 1

The chaliss of Shakespeare's hell verses' visions
Joins all timeless writers' divined perfections
Goethe's depth part II, and hell's soul-inspection
Conrad's ghost mentor tempts young directions
Homer timed learning, adventured connections

Soaring hell's powers, give in heaven's connection
Requiring instruction, save soul certification
Condemned innocence nonjudgmental redemption
While God's training damns fear's reactive inaction
So far reported that ...
Given heaven's professed costs for mildest exemption
Hell's coarsest catch wins God's higher salvation

Woven Symbols - 2

Can't develop Shakespeare's love
Of poetry and communication perfection
And Goethe's depth and perception
And Joseph Conrad's growth of youth
Maturation of an arrogant young one
And Marlow's descriptive art
And Homer's ballad of singing hearts
Can all partake of gifts?
To share and treasure life's real spirit
Severed from religious?
(Do all know hell first when asked to heaven?)

EAT CONTRASTS

Our opulence's presence
As courteous bows
Beneath the shoulder
Press
Bellies full
Resting now
To let the fat lie still
Rest
Be awake
Hunger's cry
Melt your heart
Dress, redress
In death's time

COLD AWAY

All tuned to the air
Flight has its word
Calm ever stream
Will the willow bend?
Coolness about you
Has faded away
Cropped ground
Where grass does not grow
The hostile wayside
Is here
Gone between
And meandering
Looking ahead
And my back turned

STOLEN STUDENT BIKE

One kindly bike disappeared today
And is possibly on its way
To Santa Barbara, Irvine, or L.A.
Possibly Marin, or to SF by the Bay
It was a green five-speed, my friend this Bianchi
Ten years less one it has tended my company
And my lament—the books it could carry
Speed and dead brakes—never tarry
Long trust in human character
Genuine faith in hominid honesty
Do not delay who you be
To return this cherished benefactor

ALASKAN DOCK

How pleasant it is to feel the snow
It lies on the window
It is beside me and attracts
My attention as it melts to a river
Of water trickling
Flushing down an alley
To the street where a fisherman
Gathers it up and drinks
His face glows and is pleased
He looks up and a face looks upon him
And lifts him to his feet

OLD BELL TOWER

Non cathedral
Still reverent
Non old castle
Still watching
Non firehouse
Still protecting
Non factory
Still producing

Old Plain Street
Modern value
Old marking
Modern tourist
Old dress shower
Modern wedding
Old horse trail
Modern convoy

Sierra cross-over
1800s–2000 plus
Sierra Hangtown
1800s–2000 plus
Sierra wagon train
1800s–2000 plus
Local gold mines
1800s–2000 plus

Central tower
Gathers crowds
Central old town
Gathers veterans
Central cheer
Gathers New Year
Central arts
Gathers vineyards

Hangtown tower
Bell rings music
Hangtown tourists
Bell times maverick's
Hangtown carriage
Bell marks loading
Hangtown center
Bell's revolution

Chimes' sung phrases
Describe charm
As historians
Describe hung men
As railroads travel
As describes labor
As describes progress

Memories given by Chinese, Japanese, Native American,
Irish, Mormon, Mexican, Spanish, Scandinavian,
Russian, French, British, and more

ONCE QUESTIONS OF IDENTITY

Announce
>Who am I?
>>I am the Service
>The Service
>>A park's service
>I serve.

Who?
>I serve
>>I am not sure ...
>>There's no item—
>>>isolate
>Yes,
>I serve the people

Serve the people?
>I serve the people
>>Do I draw, impersonate?
>>—by offering a future.
>I serve the people
>>Options
>>Offering them a future.

You are whose?
>Whose am I?
>Yours.

What do you give?
>Cause for pleasure.
>Where?
>>Our biosphere, our nature,
>>All constituent cultures,
>Your home's curator.

How do you serve?
>Sobered devotion
>Least intervention
>Bridge across respites
>>In time's continuous
>>Change. I know.

The present?
      Lays down in nature
      Incongruous
History's bite
      Yes,
      Competition's replay

HANDSOME—HANDSOME

Handsome, handsome
You, husband, see me
Around a kitchen's corner
Or as I leave the building
With arm outstretched
With flowered bouquet
Wrapped in foil's shimmer

Beckoning eyes
As you look at me
Red lips wishing for a kiss
Warm arms ready for a squeeze
Handsome man, I am waiting
For your memories

Chase me down again
When I see you
I look for those eyes
Your smile and bearded dimples
I look for the lips and arms
Remember as I do
The genesis of loving
And most certainly
I'll have you without
Any needs
No problems reckoning

Twenty-First Century to Its Twenty-Second Child

Was I to know that it was pain I caused you?
I'd change it all so readily
How could I know you'd miss clean air?
Or foresee your life of squalor
See it, if you can, to forgive your parents
Our benign neglect
For loss of forests, all food biodiversity
Know that your future was our only desire
See our remorse and sorrow we carry

If you only knew how busy we were
How hard we tried
How tired we were
How much we hurried

Did you know how much we saved?
"Renewable" was our affirmation
And we looked to each other for change
Knowing as we did
That we'd crushed the udder irreparably
Turning all milk fetid

After life's beauty fed us
Earth's diversity cured us
Perhaps you will see
Why it was all for the better
For us, you'll see
Now, adjust to the weather
See light through this silt
Don't sit and wonder, why?

Then, when you have time
Think of what you'll do
In doing so, remember me

MEMORIES OF YOU

To empathize your loss
I need only feel the love I have
For my family, friends, for my daughter
Or I only need to remember the sorrow
As I felt it a few years ago
At losses close to my heart
That sent deep pain
Through me, my cousin, my grandmothers
That I was grateful to know
Thankfully it doesn't occur more
That I would grieve continuously
And, thankfully, the births that occur
Give me comfort, hope
That life replaces life
Our deaths come tomorrow
For the new lives
Are free to follow
An eternity
Free of burdens
Lost vulnerabilities
Once with us
Drift to faded memory

Still and more deeply
Alive, and
At the very least
Memories cling
Our hearts see time
In fresh melts of spring
Everything to sunshine
Light passing
Through the window

Dropping buckeyes
A birth of snow
Towering red madrones
Drawn
Maple seed's wings
Fallen
Greet a winter sleep
While I, awakening, feel
Softened tears, remembering
Not mourning, all good years

MIND DRIFTS

These words are in my mind
They speak of my mind
My consciousness
And mostly the lack of it

They ramble ...
But they do not go nor fly in vain
This latter part will open
And I will know it
And grow

These are the ramblings
Of a passionate heart
Of its tangible gifts
It is the passing for life
That death has no doing with
Life leading all to know
Options will hold me

HOW MANY GOOD ONES?

How many good
How many poor
How many mediocre
    Muster quality

        I can muster
One person's verse
Other ones nonsense
What qualifies the
    Solemn?
What conveys joy?
        Which human message
Beyond one's self and to
    Another's heartfelt
Where's residual calm
When visual poems surround
Carried by stilled words
        To receiver
One to the other
Diverse

LONG TERM STATUE

Welded lips
Statue posing
Fountain waters
Bronze and rust
Lashes limping
Thinking
Life might be
Motion
Touching
Streaking time's portal

Portrayed love
Left lasting
Awaking
Quaking
Seeing grounds
Changing
Bronze lips raise
Separate
And part

Age

YOUTH

Youth is a fleeting moment
By the time it is noticed, it's gone
Youth is a moment of reject
Of the tardiness of what is to come
And once these things come
We wish they were still not yet come
In order to be what we truly are
We must not confine
To that which we were taught

GIGGLES HELD FONDLY

A room filled with all people
Yawns
A child runs, trips, cries
Yawns
Profuse among the crowd
Captured in the gate
All adorned for travel
Blue pants laced with white flowers
Giggle, laugh—hide and seek
A happy child, affectionate mother
Beautiful nose diamonds
Black floor
She grabs Mom's legs
She bites and giggles
Held fondly
She escapes
Top run to Daddy
Far on the other side
A white cap on a child's chariot
Staff resting beyond the door
It's cold out there
In here it's hot
Inside, trapped by glass doors

Teen Nose—Noisy Mirror

Nose up
Nose straight
Nose flat
Nose point
Nose beak
Nose pin
Nose button
Nose rose
Nose thin
Nose prim
Smells dim

WHEN YOUR SLING WAS CORDUROY

I remember when you were a pouch on my breasts
When, in blue corduroy, your body held snug
Your little legs hung and arm spread to the side
And your head fell to the right as you slept
As if all worries, consciousness, did not exist
And never would youth's dreams persist
Though they were there indeed

Your head fell to the right as you slept
Turning over, tucked in, "sleep tight"
Softly on your pillow, once a pouch on my breasts
Following first exploits in first grade
Read you a poem, a "Blue Guitar"
Music was slumber, dreams regard
I remember

How you still fall asleep so smoothly
When I read you "The Blue Guitar," sound
Your unconscious soared in endless directions
My affections stirred, admired your calm
Sleep and serenity while your lids laid still
While young

Then I would carry you
And do still, occasionally, too
As I would do,
From eight pounds to forty-two
Blessed sleep, still
And next day hold you
On my lap so grown
Near one decade
Later, while writing
Imagined when you're grown
Writing, "I'll still hold you"
Love

Now decades passed
Mostly into memory
Looking far back
Upon the sleep I hoped
That would remain so deep
To rest, refresh
Hoped, wishing you calmness's dream

I wrote ahead

Let no years force a stress
To which your body succumbs,
Bringing you pain, or
Leave you diminished and restless.
Let me take it all on myself in advance
So you at first, experience charm
Have access to a peaceful life
Equally, rewardingly, plan fun
Live laughter with least strife.

We can't control most events in pain
But wish options to whether they come
Not succumbing to stress that strips you
Not succumbing to prides that dare you
Pliable, letting events pass and not break you."

Life, give to my daughter,
Entice full joys of adventure
Experience she loves that lasts
While handing pipers only their shares

Tonight, I ask you, life's calm nights,
Give my daughter sleep for her dreams
Unlimited causes to smile,
Radiant love and all to nourish
Her untapped strength and growing mind

(Later to follow)

All grown, my dear
Regarding your every need
I wish most
That hardened times diminish
You still see fine; see that
All that instills pain will fall aside
Let dreams override

Confluent and overtaking
Are all best things and attributes
Yes, all rekindle, reassemble
With ephemeral tides working
Each adding layers of foundation
Impermeable to erosive back-dreams
Sums of your best visions
All dreams' rewards

May those best things and attributes
Replenish and enlighten you
Encourage you
Protecting your fondest
Ultimately most restful dreams
My love

INNOCENCE, CHARM, AND CONTAGION

It's a stuffed bear before me
It doesn't growl
And the child is frightened
"It doesn't bite me?"
Caressing stiffly
Softly caressing
And hesitating, smiling
With a doubt
A single doubt
Maybe two
Caress softens

Even a stuffed one purrs
And as he leaves
The bear sinks down
His stuffed pleasure parted
The child sees his mother leave
He hesitates
And hesitating, smiling
With a doubt
And looking back
Turns the stool

His brother comes
And slugs the bear
He looks and slugs him, too
He slugs the bear
That remains so still
Again, again, and
Slugs him
Tall thoughts distracted
By the ice cream
The lips curl
And tongue extends
To lick the next adventure

Toward the Schoolyard

It's a cool summer morning
Surreal mire-mortared drips slip away
Bowls red clay washed
Painted as Grand Canyon streams
Dropped in a sink
Sunken to clear while I awaken
I sense bites of fog draft
Pecking old, cabled windows
Showered hair combed
Braid strands dream
August parts on T-shirt
Jeans and sweat shirt
Look out through glass to morning

Grey cast on street
Poles, wires, gone lost in us
Camouflaged by water drops
Suspended in lakes, airborne
Warm currents risen, mixed in
Salted cold air
Condensed éclat of dripping salt pebbles
I descend our stairs, the street
Two flights on narrow wood
Oak creaks doused first with clutter
Of my laces still untied
Dried wood door leaks
Drafts from winds gusted, dead
Tripped by entering fogs
Its motion squeaks stress

Lunch garnished gathered
My books, daypack, my
Harnessed walk uphill
My nose, cheeks, and chin
Pink-red contrast to concrete pale
Drawn at first breath
Impregnating fog's cool, wet touch
In crossing doorsteps of crosswalks
Iron entry at playgrounds
Sunset gate slapping
Shut

I smell the breath
Of an ocean's exhale
Feel drips, wetted air
Hill winding enlivens, driven
Energy rises, lifts my smile
Disguises to drift and float sails
Unbound by weight, skims winded
Walk to school
Uphill chipper
Sand surrounds livened growth
Mosses open on rocks cluster
Layered soft earth's brethren
Dew fallen drips, trickle
Beads decor, forming streams
I enter a gate, cross the gutter
Safe entry

School rather spaced-locked
A stall
Where warm air clouds—dry
Dehydrates
The fog and my chipper smile dies
Lost fog vapors
Wood plastic desks
Dry sued, breath's taste
Blank lectures
Inside-out life's fodder
Freckled minds inside callused plates
Held by lead solder
Poisoned and bled

THEY PLAY

Incline
Rail carves
Steep ravine
Micro boundaries
Old brick
Newly paved
Bells
Ring
School begins
Pine forested
Learning cover
Yard
Children
Dance
In ball's gust
Shine lips
Cheeks
Red noses
Fog's chill
Gain vigor
Play
Pleasure
Innocent
Gathered
Childlike
Bright light
Learning
Insight
Near
Exotic
Food
Shopping pleasure
A square
With tree
Music chatter
Noel!
Real pleasure

Parents
Walk
Pick up
Pleasure
Growing child
Departing cradle

Growing visor
Love
Glad consumer
Toys
HD
TV
Hypnosis then
Luster lost
Extinguished sensors
Change
Vital love
Dimensions
Change
Undefined
New described
Observed
Teen's rage

GENERATION'S GENEALOGY

Generations back, we separate
    The origins from different seams
Generations back, our families
    Collide and recourse
In fine detail—in times
    Widening observers' tones

Translated stories pass to
    A beginning, gliding
On information regarding
    Retentions
The fog broadens more so
    Widely as time regresses
Broader and more obscure
    Lifts items and detail

Long time memory
    From record drawers
Separate names divided
    From origins
Divided and differed
    Over generations
    Exponents of time

MY KID: LOUVRE AND RED RIVER GORGE

Have you ever raced though beauty?
Like the Louvre in fifteen minutes
Or Red River Gorge in twenty?
That insatiable thirst for speed
... suggests your smile
"That's all this child needs!"
My daughter, you're speeding

DAILY TIDES—MATERNAL PATERNITY

Swollen ankles
Desk or café leg trousers
Stranded, visualized
Sits longing
Conducting speaks
    Back dropped
Avid motion lands
Feet—dead flat energy—time tops
Awaiting charm and smile
My child's smile
Seeming far
Woven, timed from
    Breakfasted work and grocery
Shop priorities to my child time
Hours—depart—disappear
Every time
    Competes the quality in moments' pile
Reaffirms qualified mentality
Confined outside
Repealed inside
Gibbered splendor
Missing
    My baby's smile
Tossed tax, billing forms
Succeed slumber
A child's smile, mine
Sung slumber rhythms
Sung, spoken waves
From "Blue Guitar"
I remember
Choice times
Bedtime stories
Evenings' charmed utters
Dishes washed
Papers fed
TV gone
PC recline

Rescreen
Revise
My bed is empty
The udders hide
Dreams miss me
Morning lifts wakened gifts
My child smiles
Off to work
Daily tides

First Trip to the Sea

Small, white, new pink feet
Looking at five toes
Cement's reflection and
Wet hair dripping
Seashells
Homeless snails
Clamshells comparing
Blue, black, violet
Wet trunks
From bathing drenched
Glossy hair cleansed
    From sea
Rinsed by sand
Small suit covered with flowers
Young body looks
On young feet
Small steps
But masterful splash
Peas in a pod
Saltine
Good breakfast and dinner
For young water's great pleasure

WALKING TO THE FRONT DOOR

I see your anticipation
Excited expression
And feet running
Small body following
Trying to keep up
With its lower half's pace race
Jump with elation
Inquisitive remarks
Tightest hug
And tug
Kissing my cheeks
Pulling my hair
For balance
With "What is it, Mommy—what did you bring?"

The Child That Ran

The child that ran
      With all her friends
Grew
Still running as if to catch
      The rainbow's treasure
Fast
Might the prize fly?
      And disappear in
Sunshine
Blond laces turned to a
      Woman
Songs
In my mind's memories
      She grew and blossomed
Free
With the humming bird
      On the wing
Carries all poetry with
      Growth's ontogeny
Serenity

MISS YOU

You're in my heart, and I miss you
The distance between us cannot last too long
For you love me and your Domi
And we both adore you
She holds you
I caress you
We live for your love
Sweet man, we miss you
      Smiles and sweet mischief
Grins 'round mustache that
      Brightens our day
Booby in courtship
      Your dance is unique
My daughter your cherub
      Coyly tests Daddy's humor
"I want a green one, no, a blue one,
      And one for Mommy, too!"
Daddy, she loves you, misses you, needs you, wants
To embrace you, cuddle you
And I do too
Hurry

Good-Feeling

Maturing
  I am maturing
The thirst for learning and open mind
To grasp at thoughts to starving minds

I see the light; it says "reach for me"
No answers but fulfillment it provides

Stretching out
Beyond safe horizons
As sunsets melt and new days awaken
Passing stars that sweep the night's dream

Maturing in love of moment
   Of soul and body
Growth so quiet and unrelenting
My (your daughter's) life progresses

Youth's Knots

Share our thoughts, you and I
Develop our souls mutually
See life together
It seems a pity to have so much
Kinship within our confines
Love's minor brain and grinding wheels
Producing the dust that collects
Over them in disguise
I want to understand
Can we get there somehow?
Can you show me?

CLEANSING TIMELESS SLEEP

Eastward we watched lavender light the sky
Snow peaks are distant but send us perspective
      on distance, size, and majesty of many qualities
Fall mists of cold air, waking valley waters draw peace
      even as we feel the freeze biting our cheeks

Life stirs and wakes despite making protests
So lifted by the wings of egrets, herons, loons, up to raptor
heights
      life feels free, we're unbound
Our thoughts see down, past our fences, our walls—enclosed shut
doors
When lasting unconstrained, we moved well across

A moment feels no restraint, there stresses slip off
      clipped by each other, dropping like cockroach skins
Failing to camouflage springs coloration, feeling change
We felt change

Envelopes from life's domain, shrinking matter's tomorrow's
horizon
Thought and emotion stretch
Feathered wings drop
Suffering shrinks to the imperceptible, beyond even artists'
views
Binding sorrow lifts, opening my spirit once again

Have you heard the meadow lark sing to the horizon?
Such an endless valley land
Space seems infinite at this time

Rocking and every night's tale—they were there
Never failing to rock my child and invite her dreams to carry her
Wherever she would go

See Her Go

See her go
See my child
It's my little one, not me, not us
New life that stirs
Grows up
She'll miss all the identity stamps
She'll be her own and smart
When we hold or corral her spirit
Energy penned
Fights back
Spunk and finesse
Way has her leading
Standing up there
Seeing the hill goes on
Valleys don't stop
Hold her from cutting paths
Moving weakness, fights, sprints
Calling motive birth
Back, back again
Weakness converts to strong
She's come
One along
Up way come a long way climbed over scooped mounds of dirt

2-25 Years Later Loved One

(2 years)
Goodnight
Slumber's on your angel's face
Peace at rest upon your pillow
Sleep, dream of youthful days
Sleep softly, rosy cheeks
Lashes lovely, placed positions
Each lash an artist's pen
Soft forehead
Dream on child
As I hold you tightly
In my arms

(25 years)
Remembrance draws me
To you dear, so far away
So near
Dreams move me closer and closer
To you so taken
Intensely resting

Times Passed for Us

There is a man, I knew him well
And yet he'd been mystifying
Brilliant and seen insight
Put him far beyond my eyes
Something magical seen about him
And I'd ventured to understand
But it would be many more years
Another morsel would reveal
He'd not been beyond all faults
His mystic qualities weren't binding
Memories sedate, not saying much
Still, blessings shared and managed
They withstood old life's withering

ONE DYING

She's dying
As youth grows
With roped hair
Braided hair
Tomorrow
Is awaiting
Tomorrow is coming
Searing her skin
Time
Clouded
Winded
Mixed realization
Spent expectations
Return and replay

MY LAP—MY BABY

My lap my baby
Six years old
I hold your warmth
Hands pulling my hair
Continuous motion
Energy
Energy
Continuous motion child
Tug earrings
Wiggles, pulls, climbs, and descends
On and off
Lean backward and forth
Where is the little
Apricot bottom
Cherry-like lips
And peach-freshened cheeks
Eyes are blue oceans
Lids angelic
Open affection

Health's Sanities and Insanities

Sinful Breach in Weight Loss

A sittin' here
A digestin'
Food goin' down
My intestine
Happiest thoughts
Cross my mind
And twixt my teeth
And palate behind
I savor

RECURRENT BREACH IN WEIGHT LOSS

And when that fish bone
Lies behind the
Potatoes that must have
Made the dinner
Without the meat, though
I fed the joy that
No waste has
Occurred for
I have eaten it

GAVE IN

Holding back
Carved in sugar
When on track
Not home

Diet stance
      knocked out all
      routine

Two hours in advance
One half-hour gone
Errands moving
Cast away
True distraction
Food attraction

Diet stance
      give myself all
      remorse, but to eat

Thursday forced
Lax of measured progress
Strength

AUTISTIC RUST

Gaze at pallets, touch the stands
    Query sight from air
Surface motion, paint restrained
    Edges merge in pairs
Tracked boundaries cross the planks
    Never touching skins
Lines weld a sane man's bond
    Lettered battle pins
Fluttered movement seems a mess
    Gasping air sacs drop
Multi windowless
    Seeks foundations' clocks
Invasive presence on motion's ride
    Touching as if dead
Encrypted perceptions omitting time
    Volume's life cut thin
Distance marked by magnets' fields
    Volted edge defined
Where power skips, skin has fled
    Sensory lines give out cut
Perception rests in motion's tires
Stayed points round about
    Overlap
Time bisects, events fire

ROUGH

Leaning memory abstained grace
Clever an enemy of sphinctered race
Lying epiphany else's storm erase
Defining blow left-sided dead embrace
Scurry warrants regal glow
Sandy cornfield revered no
Softened siphon cesarean know
How not to revel and soften row
Stream's river gas lion face
Demeaned, raised, dead, erase
Gone with wind-plagued waste
Forecasts of future weather rotten face
Seeing love redeems song's float
And inked weary defining wet soap
Pleased and brightened defining blow
Now soot replaces risen loath
Given chance and breath
Respired soul's castle
Starts moat's race
Autism's walls, spire surface bends
Airy limbs, panel's margins

DYSLEXIC—EPILEPTIC TEASE

Does the dyslexic
    See her name
    Placed twice
        In the frame
        Of a poem?
Does she see
    The stumbling
        Nature
    In the frame
        Of her prose?
Dyslexic tease
    Mixed with pain
    Young memory
        Lost heart
        And personality
Dysfunctional two
    Two identities
    One's formality
        Other's sobriety
        And care
When the distance
    Regalia
    Speed parts
Garner distance for
    Memory
    Recognition
    Memory
The names mix
    Losing identity
    Losing sobriety
    And patience
Heartfelt loss
    Parody of
        Recognition
        And cosmetic
        Humility

To without other's self
    View
        By two
        Mixed identity
One's love
    One's profession
    Fatality
    Dyslexic hibernating
With this epileptic sinews
    Semi-seizure moments
    Dissected
    Forgotten
Mixed with personality
    Conscious blending
    Fixing focus
    Mortality grace's favor
    Gratitude
Send me forward
    Aspiring forward
    Integration
    Seeing eternal
    Respiration and recognition
Post a page or
    Two paragraphs
    Losing hands
    Lay ability
    Translate thought
    To letters or
    Any formality
Knowing all "A"
    "aaaaa,aaaaa-a…"
    lines
    Infinite string
    Stretched letters
    Render a pantomime
Humor as presented
    Made naked
    Losses forestation
    Strictly uphill run

Conveying disconnected
    Morsels
    Seeing lost
    Seeing dense
    Where in fact
Brain's open space
    Open space
    Opens spacious paths
    Where seizures travel
    Where dyslexia more
    Not to mention
    Lyme beast's morsels
Without atoll
    Bridges
    Or interference
Passage is clear into
    Eternity
    Past earthed
        Dimensions
    Some reality
    Reused
    Redefined
    For clarity
Transmissions dement
    Spirochete kisses
    Spiritual events
    Lyme-twist limbs
    Cut minds and bodies
        Cut energy
Hopeless, hopeless, constant
    Apology
    To a body
To a mind

KILL THE PAIN

Sway me
Caress me
    My same pain
Cuts my spine
Love me
    But don't pity me
My wish wants your love
Let me feel you
    Hold me
Let us tangle in your grasp
Help me cut this crisis
Kill the pain
Remove my back
Remove my head
When my body rejects me
It would have me do nothing
Caress me
When I hurt
Let me function
Let me sleep
Let me be normal
Without pain
Love me, but don't pity me
Feel sorry, but don't withdraw

Seizure's Usual

My view is smaller
As my head contracts
Preparing
As interior pressure
Pushes against the soft skull
And throbs away
Knowing what's next
And a current of stillness
As thumping
As thumping marks our
Way through as
If the feeling could be postponed
And prospected happiness
Sees its way through
To the end of this one
To the last at all
And the time while we wait
For the guidance
We'll wait for your arms
To grab our hearts
Vigor as I lose my words
And write nothing
As I lose power
      Over this play's episode

GRAINS IN SAND

Grains in sand
Repeated verses
Themes
And observations
By artist's eye
Millions?
Trillions?
They use in parable
One certain truth
Lost in nature
Sand is ground
Mobile dune
White from lives
And shells so strewn
Fragments from pressures
And ocean surf's breaking
Gentle progress
Geologic bliss
To a moment's eye
And human refrain
As it sifts through
My hand

I forget my pain
Spasms
And cramping
Endless wrenching
From something vague
Coral toxin
Cells enhanced
My saline veins

Grains sift smoothly
Loose finger grips
Caressing softly
An endless cry
From my hand
Of life's fragments
Nacre and limestone
Limestone and nacre
Changing endlessly
Floating reliever
Dozing off
Finally swell

SEIZURE'S WORD: "ACCOUNDING"

Note: This was written during the seizure. The language is typed as it was written. The handwriting seems very normal—the words are not.

There were moment when the feeling sent
    Where sent there is our time
    Where we could consider fonder
Here we would the *vounterings*
    There in the time that the changes
    The thoughts send the want
The soft time *emeverint gueses* rest on *verume*
    Gone for the *mome tunty*
    There gone for some quiet moment
Gone to faith
Gone to help
Sleep

AFTER TOMORROW (BRAIN SURGERY)

The day after tomorrow I'll be out again
How will I feel the calmness of here?
What should I remember?
That can redress the cuts off my brain
The tensions, stresses and insane calm
There must be some view, different one
Given through modified lenses
Something of seeing and memory
More than other things to remember
That will be clear as the water
Colorful as a reef or great rapids
Lively as the spirit here—I wonder
What something keeps me alive?
What is it, what shall it be who I am?
I'm being swamped with states-revised
Stimulation's offerings
What's their kind?

CORAL POISONING

Though I have to keep trying
Pain moves me on
What time is passing?
I am motionless
Pain forces me on
Don't let it pass without leaving me free
I keep trying
I force my body to ignore
Smiling in adversity
Keep your arms
Your love about me
That my life will someday
Taste its freedom.

Polarized

Polarized
Mesmerized
The loss of no grey
Middle way
Bear to the death
The bed's not made
Polarized
Mobilized
Sinking
Mesmerized

SEIZURE'S WORDS: DOING HELP

Life spreading across our dwarf
Soft imagination to natural aids
Depends on loss and care
Brought to have and care long determine
Animation and sitting to find future
Soft separation of ability
Separation during spell
So difficult to separate *leletote* when *minde* and help and
Mind is working mind without full knowledge of *septege*
And futures knowledge of mind separate by help!
If only my mind were clear, always free of effects
No need to worry of knowledge
Stable of future and present knowledge
Glass green meadow which in fluid
Signals to the sun's reflection
A spectra mirror wave motion
Yellow scales that stir as feet pedal their wake
A fir of masts from dense harbor members
Looking on as protruding whiskers tilting
Muscle movements
Sidewalk embossed with green edges
Where foot prints don't tread
And bordered by fenced bridges of marina

LOVE SONG AT THE SEA'S BEACH

Remember me at the office
      When you are on the phone
Or when you're at home
Whenever frustrations mount fast
      And filled with trepidations
Stop and remember me

My seizure's sin
Calm and uprooted
In pleasant repose
Drifting in space

There, lying down
Under sun, wind
Drifting sands, resting
Remember

All recollections
Are the same
In temporal disconnections
Forever real
Whether calm or "insane"

Au/Rtistic Dimensions without Space

Eyes gaze the palette
Eyes touch the painter's stand
Eyes quarry sight from airs around
And paint moves surface gone
Across space, hands merge
Terraced boundaries always crossed
Never touching, non-descending, none crossing
Linked strokes flutter
Within lines—skin moving reflects/as minor
Houses drawn plans
Multidimensional pane wide range touch
Sealed foundations merge
By air joining matters shrivel invade
Invasive motion of touching skins
An edged painting displays
Encrypted perceptions
Free of constrictions
Expanded dimensions
Omitting time
Omitting surface
Or volume confines
Perception of movement's actions
As the life platform
Non-confined and stymied
Means loss of erosion
Spirit dead in squares
Closeted boxes
When expanse is bare
Reverence marred
Old rules, old spires
Spread when life embraces new
Aromatic ecstasies
Spirits graph iron and souls aspire

TICK'S TOCK STOCK—CYCLE FULL CIRCLE

From the twenties, still in school

My Lyme's and epileptic gridlines
Caught in life's coarsest filter
Gridlines come gridlocked
Though still I see

Life climbs, lusting lunge of dagger pains
Set sorrow festers, feeds depressing grains
My-grains, migraines, epileptic aches hang lost
Fraught maternal helplessness

Daughter at seven, I'm thirty-eight

My greatest ones, close, I love upmost
The worst demonic passed on to you
Another tick's fated bite, time's demise
Fraught pain, drowns innocent laughter
Compounds sorrow, anger, and doubt
One at seven, I'm at thirty-eight

Why life retains life, inhuman struggles
Why not gift a merited life?
Earned persistence, learned resistance
Yearns real food, movie, and pleasure
Housing expense, net income
Hard work depreciative pay remains

She's twelve, and I'm forty-three

My daughter's Lyme's ranking pain
Pry loose independence and pleasure
Give my dear daughter
Give my dear daughter , and I
Relief?

Have Lyme recant, repay, reverse
        its damage
These years' defeating struggles
All recurrent degenerative packs
Energy, pain, lost concentration, pain
Sports remained terminated

I in my forties, she's still young
I lost
Doors locked jobs constrained
Trust sickened distrust's imagination
Taken, adding pain
Pills for kill, worked skill

Politics' laughter, logic's gait
Deceptions scores of wanton causes
For ascribed efforts' displeasures
Deny gains, measure physical losses

Memory scars, lessened lost sleep
Carving deep through vulnerable sites
Spirochetes, medical ignorance,
CDC sleeps, observation fries
Objectivity marinates

Threats from jealousy macerate
All self-esteems in death of ranks

She's in college, I'm watching from
        a distance

Two years added following
Student playing, sleep defying
Spiral cheats lay waking, wanting
Acting, expanding, reproducing

Vomits drowning lecture breaking
Falling out, loosing track, yet no slack
Determined value struggled climbs
Straight-wall timed events

Sick, pained, Lyme-warped
Squelched strength, spirochete atrocity
Pills for kill, for pain, for skill
Melts dark, soiled, poisoned fodder
Times refrain, grown strengths drained

Plastic life's randomness shows
Borne blanket slow repose
Consistent with life
I cry asking exception
Wanting exception, recognition
Support my daughter's
Election to strengthen

Loosen languish, spill soul's strength
Exhume, rebirth all lost successes
Repair, sweeten crossed trails
Release her life
Return confidence, joys refrain

Hope, use strength
Relaxation unsmothered
Redundant reversals for setback
Feedback, releasing time, unlimited goals
Engaged choices and capturing prime

Reward her strengths, her dispersions of pain
Regain her life's independence, joy's essence

Sunk in a maternal mud wallow
Weak, self-pitied, helpless, fallow
Mothered hopes of sealing over
Innumerous carcass graves
Time's pain, deplete, delete, repel
May gifts opportune show you dear
Tangible success and splendid passage
Within youth's bounds, not waiting later

Opportunities selective in cold real literals
Ignorance by loose links to definition strong
Loose links to wit, slackens courage
Time links dulled past to self sinned regret
At weakest strengthless, mother watching

Wanting drawn focus,
Wanting eyesight's recognition
Rewards for sole daughter

Unyielding tensors catch, fight hell
Risk and trial, twins in pressure
Scaling freedom, rare envy
Labor blossoms curiosity

Momentarily, permanently?
Now reclaims health's newest pain
Regain time, others' expectations
Archetypes, scale cycles
Measures refrain losing
Conventionally poured restrain
I see you suffering, but not the Lyme

Once again, you grip and gain
I see you compensate
You see yourself reclaim
Calm, I couldn't be prouder
Strength, only sober

We give applauding sounds
As you break through
Years of dark competition
In other's dimmest worlds

See hopes, elations, delivered
Loving banquets to your wishes
My strongest courageous daughter ...
Daughter 's twenty-five, and I at fifty-six
Moving on

Real food, expense met income
Independence, pleasure
My dear one daughter
Fought years earning, succeeding

Twenty-seven and soon fifty-eight

Daughter drives spirochetes own plunder
Non-succumbed, worst overcome
Though damaged needs
We need her, and she needs most
Generous moments, generous gifts
All more generous than you think
Should be there, aware, and see
Fairly your gifts and earned insights

When literally engaging in
Flagellating battles
With medical corners
Remedial demeanors

Blinded cameras
Lying in Lyme's blood
Dilemma and pain
As you try, try, try, you try
tried, gained ... and moved on

... So far, after

Let it be, let it be
Ticks demolished
Pains diminished, brain cranking up
Perked as seven-year-old's slick mind
Painless unscolding golden smile
Incessant pranks and laughter
Return to her, to my daughter
Some twenty years after,
Better than we could ponder
Release for this young woman
Her dreams and wondrous times

Epileptic Eulogy or Epilogue

I'm sorry as I watch the sun pass by
It's dreary thinking of days gone by
They're weary of watching weeks
If only the fairies, wish I'd dream
A wish for a change or I'll wilt
Mind in an end's full range
Free me from this confine?
Forever to plea the Divine
Begging a clear breath
Cool, free, clear, and fine

A wish for an open eye
Do not let my mind die
If I could regain my strength …
Could you let me just express?
In clear air, with clear words
All in sequence, selected
I'll fight, push, and pull free
With a determinate strength
That, say my seizures, good-bye!
I reply: "Do not let my hope die"

First Sight: Lights Fly

Lights blink in the corner of my eyes
Chopped light, pulsed, disappearing
Like a tropic scene or wonderland
Am I seeing? Seizure or firefly

Firefly, you're not a fly, but a beetle
Not fire, but you have contained reactions
That chemically ignite your life
And pluck reactions from my eyes

Why do you pretend?
Things you have never been
Or is it that my tag on you
Light's fallacy and pretense in words

That you fly with wings is proper
But you have two wing-pairs, and a fly has one
Your outer ones are hard and sturdy
When the flies two wings are soft and fragile

The excitement you stir, especially
To this newcomer, is brilliant
And in eastern woodlands surprises me
In D.C. gardens finding you, real, no misnomer

Having injured my head
Seizures imbed, arms tied to crutches
Not hallucinating? Am I?
You are lit my firefly, flying by?
One blink says, yes.

REGENERATIVE HIGH[10]

I feel very strange
I think it is a surge of overwhelming joy
And yet my eyes are crying, wet with tears
It's often that these feelings come
These highs, but it's been half a year since the last
I'm so happy, euphoria, seizures die
Feelings of serenity
Objectivity and harmony
For not only perfect beings
But simple ones like me
Fortunate

10 Written when, after brain surgery, I had no seizures for ½ year, and was driving again.

DEAR FRIEND

What are the thoughts, feelings?
A good and very fine friend has said a good-bye
In ways so indirect
Its effect is heavy, sensations of tight joints
Dry ligaments, stiffness, and no pleasure
He's losing strength, my friend
Old and fondest mentor
His sigh is one that takes care
To face the pending and almost
The mortar that will hold headstones
That will mark graves
He sounds like he takes death
But asks his horseman to move on
It's not time yet
His tone softens in reckoning
He thanks one friend's caring
He states valued friendship
Peacefully, thanks for it
Still seeming strong
With a weakened voice
Within the weakened case
Surrounding the strongest mind
And man
I feel his words closing the seams
On the dress worn by destiny
Inevitable stream to elsewhere
My friend might die, too soon
I feel his heavy step as he walks
Quietly on, to rest, to read
To accept moving on
The sound of death, moving on, departing on
Fine friend—looking forward to your call
For lunch, for a good talk
On particles, light, streams, authors
And history
We said, "In one month or two"
... Ourselves knew well

A SITTING—AFTER CLEANING THE TRAIL

Here I sit in times of need
Upon the battered trees
Neatly set with twined string
And stretching over the vide

The T.P. of necessity
Is laid here beside me
Strung out and neatly peeled
The tidy rolls of "Z"

So carefully built this sit-mobile
Construed so ingeniously
I await with warmth another spree
A gracious trail's cleaned latrine

FIFTEEN YEARS' SPAN

Limbs from limbs daily
I feel ripped from my body
As the pain claims my lower left half
With silent words I cry for a friend
Come, don't pity me, but hold me
So the pain doesn't claim me entirely
As I cry only my heart sounds stillness
And flea comes
"Man's my best friend ... and woman, too"
It's going away
"Paid my dues" for this half hour
For this half hour
Letting it all hang out

WORD-FATIGUE

Shelves with books with pages with words
Which of these has most meaning?
Who is the one of original thinking?
That my spirit may find life refreshing
So was the day in that world go
So faraway
Safely hidden
If hiding is such that it can be done
      So effectively
None will pass
And words will pour
Give array
Search for words
Some meaning
Set a new day
I'll think clearly

LIVE PARALYSIS, LOU GEHRIG'S DEATH RELEASING

As you lie there on the softest bed
With cover gently placed to your stationed head
Fetal skeletal porcelain body
Fragile
And breaking a yet strongest prison
I see you inside
Mind alive
Peering through large cavities
Sockets for eyes

Alert
Yet still
In paralytic dispose
Fatigue from life's struggle
To move to be free
Hands that imagine
Imagery gripping
Trying to climb out
Of this casque
A body dying
A spirit desiring

Gentle woman
You deserve better
Best of care gotten
Your loving spouse
His chagrin, pain comes
Cleaning your bedridden sores
Skeleton on sheets

Beautiful fairy trapped inside
Trying to climb out
Trying to shout
    "I live, I love, want and feel
    Do not abandon
    My human feeling
    Do not forget
    That my eyes *do* see
    Ears *do* hear
    And lips *would* move
        If they could"
As he responds, caressing
She responds, wordless
    "I love you"

Metal Wings

SECURELY WELL FASTEN

"Securely fasten well your seats ...
Please, to your seats!"
Rain's come down
Show covered cloud
Proud flights climb
So sit you down
At your row

From such fun
Overeating fleeting
Still unwounded gums
Waist-fully fattened waistlines
Fasten meat belts as you can

MYSTIC JEWELS

Off
Speed
Plane alighting
As we leave
Mystic jewels
Lights of
Night sky
Subside
Under cloud
Silver wings

12:50 FRANKFURT

The captain comes
And his assistant
At least twelve crew members
Sit on benches
So much gear
Tightly packed
Efficiently prepared
Flight's experiences
Shiny black shoes
Knitted tights
Reading books
      With yellow pages
White jacket speaking
Child still laughing
Murmur of voices
Picks up as the clock's
Time is 12:50 in line
Three little children
A red dress with black dots
A pink jacket with ponytail
Green and grey vest
The four-year-old
Leaves
And pink jacket like
My child
Six, maybe, looks on

Adult brown jacket speaks
Quietly intermittent words
To blend hair and black jacket
And white shoes
As the grey belly looks on
Now quietly
He let it all out and resigned
To destiny
Awaits the flight
A light blue sweater

With light complexion
Crew cut
Serious gaze walks by
Looking straight at the plane
To the window walks
Blue coat stands
Outside the inner door
Looking on with mustache gaze
Wondering and retreating
Walking out
To the other door
It will soon be boarding time

VORACIOUS APPETITES

Voracious appetites
Whetted
From vacated minds
Feeling rest
Free thoughts
Responsibility names
If temporarily
Follow young ghosts of air
Water solicits
Air sublime
Witness love
Witness separation
All in stride
Pride removed
Walking not sulking
But free, not dull
And seeing tomorrow
Pleasure
As it were today

The Race

White lines on blue with white patches
Blue lines on white with blue patches
Detaching
As bodies are parked
Sardines
Canned
And fermented fruit
For the picking
Littered white spots
On blue carpet
Such narrow escapes
As hips press on shoulders
Racing down a hall
Corridor effacing
Succulent shapes
And thirsty skin
So many hope they will win

AIRFLIGHT'S FACILITIES

Airplane bathrooms
Closet station toilets
Two for the trip
Made for the masses
Designed nil-class
No paper towels
No soap
Toilet paper used
Ready, on the floor
Takes charge

Papers cling
Away from water
Having missed the drain
Prior miss-fired trial
Claimed the frame
Disclaimed
We're left to seek
All residual
Any more
Sanctimonies
Wait for the door
Clean home standing
Traveling and any more
Residual sanctimonies

Waiting
All for destined airports
Hopping quickly
Walking swiftly, breathe
There we cleanse
Better an airport
Thoughts there seem
Kept clean or automatic
So seems, not here

LANDING HOME

Seeing you
Will you be there to greet me?
I've waited for this
It's coming quickly
Rejoining
Holding
Not parting again
Exchanging
Speaking
Crying with love
To be with you once more
So distant, never new
You were, never guessed
Time could be so slow
Away from home
Good work, come here
Thank God though
To be home
Three weeks, seems thirty
Long time
Home again
With you
Never again so far

IN LINE WAITING

Today is yesterday's evening
Now there is tomorrow morning
We will join from separate sleep
Exchange fondness from far
After waiting so long
In line
To be calling
Hurrying home
Reaching
You

CLOUD COVER

Cloud cover
Hovers
Over land
Expanse
Eyes
Spanned
Forever
Space
Between
Us
Ground to sky
Atmospheric
Dust

MIGRATION

Flight of flamingos
        To Venezuela
Flight of the dolphin to
        Ocean swells and
Journeys of men, women, and children
For roosting and breeding
        And weather's convalescence

Mile upon mile—through wind
        And summer thunder
Over white-crested waves that
        Carry us under
Tough currents and moon's rise
        Unchanging shades

Strong the pulls and tides
        As we wade
Across opportunity from
        Acquaintance and revelry
Hello! We're there, our
        Yearly journey
We're back to resume
        A heavenly party

WHITENED CROWS

Black silhouettes, these grey and black forms
Fly against the cumulus clouds
 "Hear me, hear me, others hear me!"
All in deep, pure tone cry
Swarm through branch and a tropic's leaves

I wonder what they see in night that makes them caw
So persistently in their sound
Communication's net-fields strange
Through winding canopies of brown
Now 6:20 melodies set in
—Of songs and hymns from
Temples sent to lovely souls

Forested peace sets in, I hardly see
Just enough to put my thoughts to pen
Soundless melodies drift toward home
Whisper to you, wishing you were here
With me so far, this far

PLANE NOTES IN MIDAIR

Soaring as they do, the brown-winged master held the air still
Plucking at its prey midflight
White object
Rodent, swift, no support
Sleek head folds like dough
Smooth movement on light wings
Tail of a Japanese fan held in a ballet
Plucking at its prey
Brown head of milk chocolate of varied tones
Varied sonnets to its breakfast sent
By circling swifts mobbing
Hounding in simulated feeding
As they would insects catch
Feeding whole, wholly, and holy
They are like the master's wing
Folding smaller life into its cycle
In midair

On The Plane—No Number

Green caterpillar moving
        Legs unseen
Windowed seats for inner beings
        Feed on asphalt leaves
They multiply, emptying their bowels
        Before each plane
And the ladder's like a feeder
Gathering food and tossing it inward
        To the beast's gross belly

Circling Delhi, we see
        Pavement rippling
Landing strip meets an
        Opened door
Stairs locked, and
        Gun barrels point
Dry water's well denied
        Docked hoses dry

Docked, out of gas
        Machine guns point
Secured, sardined humans
        Sweat shut in
Sun's crescent heat
        Canyons calm
Forced status and
        Stratus around

Atrophied limbs and
        Powerful wings
Against the haze of Karachi's
        Shade of green
Voluptuously seen life
        Against serenity

The desert brush
    Meet deserts lush
Lay along whitened
    Blue skies
A hot sun shining
    Burning through

Demanding a place
    In the flight

Opened door with steel
    Stairs locked
Dry water's well denied
    Docked hoses
Machine guns point to
    "Secure"
Sardine humans'
    sweat shut in
Sun's crescent heat, forced calm

Four hours pass by
    The plane lifts off
Flies on, one unforgotten
    Unreal December
Distanced December's day

CAN YOU FEEL?

Can you feel anything?
      Less than overtaken
When you fly into smog
      And the world below
Is beyond reach
Guts' thin layers
      When we enter
From migration land on earth
      Some other Earth
      Part of Earth
Somewhere I wish while
Absorbed in its condition

DISTANCE DISSOLVING

The journey westward is quite long
And leaves me in the quiet sound
Off breeze's hum as it cross the land
Soothing sleep, restless grass hums

I left my love away
The dream imprints on ideals
Detaches from reality
Steadily dreams move on
Cross plantations, dancing rivers
And farther my love stays behind
What is left is memory
Realities of past days
In my mind, sleep

Thoughts pass forgotten
In the wake of distance passing
Leaving lost sounds
Between our times
Between us

Do not forget me and I'll not you
Let us defeat that rotted fate
Let me leave it in the wake
Of distance passing between us

232

3,000 CLEANSES

That you are so far from me
At home, while work takes me
Few weeks seem long
Miles away, 3,000
As cloud corridors pass
Separate you from me

Love you see
On the ocean front
Meets crashing waves
Love you see
A moist, cool spray
Cleanses the skin of my face
Freshens my heart
Sensing peace, glimpsing
Sorrows with the tide
Reveals loss, love

And our child
Our greatest love
What doesn't she deserve?
Shouldn't she have?

You continue—impervious
Cold felt in tropic corals
Should you see?
Should you feel?
I weakening
Needing your support
Worse come to worse
We die, real or metaphor

And our child
Our greatest love
What doesn't she deserve?
Shouldn't she have?

Nourished future
Blossomed curiosity
Capable, expansive
Born, grown lessons
  ... more than
A hopeful love
Between us
Not lost love
  ... feeding
Lessons we've learned
Experience we've grown from
Successes we've had

And our child
Our greatest love
What doesn't she deserve?
Shouldn't she have?

Ocean spray sends salts
On another plain grass grows
  from the moisture
  from the soil
Given by the ground I so love
Beneath your feet cherish?

And our child
Our greatest love
What doesn't she deserve?
Shouldn't she have?

A Bird's Flight

As the bird soars calmly over the states
The river moves with deliberation through rocky gorges
California, Nevada, and Utah pass
And the eastern shore waits
Swiftly, I fly upward over clouds that oversee
The doings of men, gods, and mountains
Cumulus nimbus as your name foretells
What thirst will you quench, which famished valley?
Over Colorado, Nebraska, and Iowa
Clear skies cast no shadow and the wells are dry
Lastly to Indiana, worlds never seen
By these narrow eyes of this naive beholder
What wondrous land!
That—awe-inspired
I stand, waiting for more
Yet, alas, we land

STARLIGHT, STAR FLIGHT

Early on my way to work near sunrise
I look toward Orion
To the pale blue or grey sky that is morning
Across all world evening and open skies
Galaxies absorbing stars

Massive clouds ... See
Orion surrounded by the stars
In contrast to day-lit sky
Free and casting dark's light
Distinguished from daylight
Massive clouds hold you
Upon us seen
Dubbed, awesome, respect
I'll see the spot, your night sky
In my mind's imagination
I'll see Orion tonight

Shall say hello at night's moment
Tin clear starlight stargazing
Anxious for tonight, flying
No clouded, blanched urban sky
Far whitened mesh, distilled
Flown far behind, wings' eyes
Tonight, Orion, you're mine

A LONG PLANE RIDE

Couples kissing
Caressing
Nails comb through his hair
Lids close
Sensations and sensuality
The look of want
Life's childish frustration
Blushing desire
Of hot love

ON LANDING

Passing buildings
As through a lens
Grey and motionless
Against an evening's horizon
Cacophonous meadowlarks
Overlapping on classic
Melancholy
The flash moves
Through the runway
To dock
As in primitive
Senseless shock
It locks and catches
Lives spilling
Out of their seats
Rushing bodies out a door
Pushing the runway
Walkway away
Here we are in New York

SWAN'S WOMB FLYING

Perfuse it was with smells of flowers
Faded smells of sweet perfumes
Smoke, heat, and humid clasp
Of closed chest in a floating crate

I saw blue sky, white dew, and cloud
Deposition of its heaviness and shroud
Closed plane compartment warms
The womb of a flying young swan
Of humans as batches of young
Growing, moving, sweating, smelling
Chattering loud, as they cluster in situ

The swan lifts into flight determined
Time passes, the large swan land, lands, ready to birth
Setting down the runway, estuarine alley
And fluttering flushes of summer garment
All jump to fresh salted waters for a quiet soak
Feeling rested, rejuvenated, bathed
Nursed and fed by dreams' enclosures
Vacation's food and rejoined pleasures
Of home

Karachi 747

I am slowly writing as I sit here
Karachi, near India's borders
Read from a Saudi in a 747
As we see passengers very few
Luggage carried up/down
The dawn was met by the
Mist of new day—fog on the flats
Barred from New Delhi
Flat on its belly the plane lies
In the lot
Near the runway—nevermore
The air breathes clean with each draw
The barrels of this giant machine
Lie like funnels drawing our respect
Like pieces of a Saturn rocket
Domesticated for foreign flight
Waiting near the runway—forty-five minutes more
Four hours more

Can or Can't Be

5

THE OTHER SIDE

Sweltering smog falling on the whimper of crushed steeples
Once endeavored to deify open skies
The layered domain that neither God nor world want
Stays stagnant, a pool, filling with silt and eutrophic water

No Benefits of Carnage

As water drops
Floating in the sky
Bulbous like tulips
When they open
Colors of the setting sun
Or young crib's joy
Passing over my head
And getting down close to me
The carnage of the bodies
Lifted beyond the way
More than expected elation
Are photographic ecstasy
Parlay with wind and cloud
Above me below God
Seems forever free of weight
They soar beyond me
Free
As freedom comes
Beneath the clouds of taxes
Joblessness and harassed
The people bow to royalty

GIFT SHOPPING AND CRUSTED LASHES

Caked with mud
Serious eyes
Not knowing tears
Childhoods departed
Far from grown
Not questioning
Too small to go
Carrying the burden
Darts from cars
Youth and old in one
Combined
Begs for money
Carefully inspecting
Every motion
Well-dressed tourists
Traveling trios
Wealth displayed
Burdens on desire
Children's needs
Open their eyes
Not caring
Not seeming to see
"No change to spare"
Stretch out and cry
And only one dies

STOPPED CRYING

She held the child in her arms
Two legs limp, hanging down
Beneath her breasts
Child's right arm out straight
As if pointing
Directly supported by hers
Left arm dead between their bodies
Limp, head hung
The woman's sorrow
Manufactured or sincere
Or if she is the mother, regardless
The look of sadness melted me
Seeing my own arms
Seeing alternatives
Seeing my own child
Now three years
Seeing one die
I wept, soul cried
Saw the child
Head hung over
Eyes glued shut
Yellow welded secretions
Infection's oranged puss
Unconscious of her plight
As she lay limp, still as "dead"
She would die
Hopeless
Compassion's grace

OLDEST TREES THERE ISOLATED

Wandering stops here
Unlimited supply?
Earth's fresh waves
Over untrodden beach
Tall beams of green-clothed trees
Wrap bodies around precipice
They fall my eyes see
It claims my soul
It is beset with joy alone
      With sorrow
To know that tomorrow
They'll fall
Without memories of
      The souls pleased
And ashes spilt
Deaths shared in proper way
Does a gas-powered saw feel?
Like the ax or the two-man saw
      With blisters, blood
Split evenly—life for life
      And giving
That replenishment met the take?
Where are they going?

UNNUMBERED DREAM

What do you see now under the night sky?
As you look between openings in lush canopies
Where the guiding lights and shooting stars are
Between your hopes and dreams

Let's look back upon good days
To see the forest closure
And all wildlife moving in
To share the food in measure
We hear night sounds as if they're here
Without fear or inhibition
Out come flying squirrels
That complete our night's illusions

Later opens emptiness
Leaving remnant plains
Succumbed, we dispel

All introspection worthless

TRIMMINGS OF WAR

Jess got on the bus today
The sun shown all the way
Excitement building and people say
Jess's tracking home today

The sun's blazing and making it hot
Jess's coming done, battles fought
Stalled in time, the people sought
Asked if Jess was whole or not

We'd been at war now all this time
Shooting and killing, since life's a dime
Bodies thrown, covered with lime
All soldiers honored kept in line

Jess is happy, sees surviving it all
Free as a bird, flown death's wall
Now on safe ground memories call
Reminding: eat, drink, have a ball

Thought's celebration spun all wild
Parents and onlookers calm, mild
Wait watching their children file
Heroes now home no pain to recall

The bus slips on ice, meets cars head-on
Jess's riding crashes, from force rebounds
All ears heard loud, clashing cut sounds
Worlds spun former, future, time all 'round
Surviving a war, Jess's future had drowned

ENCRUSTED MEMORY

So far in sickness, in need of attention
Even beautiful in spite of her plight
Fair brown skin
God's progeny are caged in sleep
To pass on
It was too much
Too much to bear
To see her as good as alone
Knowing she'd remain in her plight to death
Never seeing doctors, as this mother begged
(I'm told not "mother" at all)
Few rupees from man to woman
To man she drew
And begged some more
While a child's fever burns
A scar marked by death
      Hovering here
Febrile child, motionless
Her tummy was like my baby's, plump
Her lips were young, little hands, little feet
Her knees were narrow
Her eyes potted shut
Glued in coma
Glued and sent to sleep

SHE'S NOT THE MOTHER?

She hung without stirring
Suspended unconsciousness
Thoughts in heaven
Already traveling
Away from fever
Pain removed
Eyes so gently shut
Not to open again
My own emotion
Gains—imagination
A mother's heart fevered

I would take her in my arms
I will have her at our home

She dies as she lays there
Strange arms hold her
Far from life
No point of reference
Just the image of innocence

Departed
Longing lost
Never returns
Just a used body
Ask "money"
With face
Frozen while
Soldered shut
For sale

All for begging
Is it real?
Is it a stranger, not the mother?
Is her heart leather?
Not yearning
Cry like mine
Is mine?

Numbed emotion
Rests in shadow
Afraid to speak
Lost ineffectual
Powerless, acts
Departed
Didn't weep?
Let her there

"Let her there, or
Be arrested"
To help recover
Conscious smiles
Fixes
Solemn stillness

Watch her die
Let it be?
My mind conflicts
Sick replies
Love denied
Mother, me
Other stranger
Festered hearts
Tourist leather
Weathered
Souls tethered
Die

Between Cacti and Wooded Streams

Far away beneath the sun where cholla grows
Beyond the horizon
A cactus blooms—a black flower at night
And its shadow rests on the moon's profile

WORLD PARK

The time's distance comes between us
Increasingly I realize what you do
To smooth and insulate world's lands
Warding off damage and obstructions
Or call, meeting entropic gains
You ignore disappointments
Energy we draw reoccurs
So many times
Within one world
Endless hospitality
Ultimate gift
So hard
Left back
Lost behind
Extermination

Past selection
Cost losses lay
Life treasures blemish
Dreams delete
Dwarf vision's love
Calmed, blinded
Civilizations replay
End your time's
Ultimate gift
So hard
Left back
Lost behind
A termination

Optimism

Slated for a Sunday's life worn layer
A sultry sun bakes red clay's fire
Young voices carry a wasted gait
All tossed food from their midst
In mass, in time
Their outstretched arms show hunger
It lingers

One soothing sunrise's soft whisper
Helps mend emotions to reconnoiter
Childhood's paths gone wrong, now repaired
Hold, damming self-justified power
Removing cold waste
Curbed losses and lasting despair for some
This time

Ixtoc-II Oil Spill

Glassed surface
     Chocolate spilled syrup
Glazed motion
     Mousses serving
Serrated floats
     Danced brown balls
Feathered motions
     Slip on plates
Tarred and tanned
     Doused in powder
Caught in sand
     Wrought starvation
Doused to anger
     Rejected nauseous
Dead enveloped
     Coastal mousse
Ephemeral life
     Crusted eddy
Cast dry, burned

CONNECT HEARTS' SORROWS - 1

What can I do when I walk?
Streets and sorrow
When older beggars grasp
At my arms
Only to find
Eyes spilling

Needs and wants
Give tender
Too little
Away from commitment
Lost

Wake hearts
Some live
More than melt

Help
Add selfless grace
Fix for the moment
Small comfort
Find the real stop
For arms let down

Love's whey conquers all
Separate so wholly for the giant

CONNECT HEARTS' SORROWS - 2

What can I do when I walk streets and sorrow?
When old beggars grasp at my limbs
Their touching fresh hands that would only give
That tours with coins, bills, all too tangent
Not related to needs, quelled murmurs of change
Do hearts find reality's tangible, edible wealth?

Views of a visitor, a spender and departure
Token anchors, sunken holds, downed depths
Wholly to the giant pour requests
Abandon's reservations set, anticipation's net
Death's cry sets its place in line, hemming hunger's dress
Sitting while watching, eyes crossing starved streets,
Counting all hands reaching for touch
Views cost food, sorrows stir pity:
Tourists hone pleasures
Sympathy mixes with empathic pity
      Cremated soot
I reek

Graffiti's Grimace

Called knives, pierce worn tires
Cramped minds sculpt deafened crews
Cut wires add one prior
Calls raise jail debts on cue

Called plights, cast dried mires
Chains disfigure, bled in views
Capped rescue, hopes fall dire
Calls fodder remnant few

Called sulfured-soot respires
Cloned gorges, gasping dews
Cupped signs, cultured gyre
Call's rap death's smoker hue

Called kills, add crime priors
Butt against walled urine spews
Kissed rides, rough smack's hire
Calls force one stagnant queue

Hazed all forage
Bled all courage
Sub- and urban scourge

Lisps of lives
Once begotten
Still forgotten
Still ignored

Meaningful-Ament

Time to go for dinner, you say
What about that child
Does she come too?

What of the who's beaten
And is scorned from affection
We bring him too?

What of the old one who's insane
And drifts and cries for notice
Will she come too?

What of the beggars
Pretending deaf and dumb
Who see you as bargains
Shall they come too?

I'll look into my food's well
It's caught by interactions
Within my soul and there
It knows, it cares

I'll cut food and press
Perhaps then see less despair?
Though I know I'm only fooling
I wish they knew I cared

Sweat through sundry mechanics
Restrain from grim views
"Where to start" forms cinders
A stifling stasis to undo

HUNGRY MICE

New time, life's good house
Shaved through clean peaks and valleys
Impressively garnered and shined our nest
Attracting attention built "family"
Clean, guarded dwellings sprawled
Each set its fashions' all-copious nest
The new ones bore more
And reshaved state mountains
Attaining foundation's all-flat décor

Emergent soon-to-be sheds
Wet mud, clung to foundations
Once refurbished, dropped demolished décor
Massed hungry modules
Now but countless, strung circles
Shade a pitted and paved, once-living place
None sold, all planned losses
Blanched, set, indebted skylights
Count values lost, collectors scrap each place

Grovel on the waste site
Shack life stands, sunken waste lands
Décor's gone, dull, owned by powdered statues
Ploughs tumble walls, en masse.
Set down endless empty fence lines
No time, spent space, lost in crusted statutes

SELF POSSESSED: DISCUSSION AND QUANDARY

My thoughts run across
      The time and temptation
As souls exchange their
      Thoughts in the room
      Grey and still
On planets future, and
      Forests that stand on mountain slopes
Our common land
      Tomorrow, terraced and trembling in fear
Of doom
Shall we deliver our own?—or other's souls
      And hearts
To society's distant clubs, or
      Shall we
—but give ourselves to here
Our local devastation, turn around
Straight on,
With local love repair them

SUNG

Young voices songs carry tomorrow's gait
Slated for a Sunday's mass and prayer
Whisper love's care, all so fondly

On a morrow's sunrise and soft, wet dew
In hunger waits all outstretched arms
City's peasants silently waste

Sultry hot sun, rendering sympathies
Bated for trembling times aware
Seer foretells tomorrow's share

FAITH TELEMARKET

Ridged thoughts
Sentiments growing
Love born wordless
Vocabulary weltering
Found in heat's work
Nude of thought and
Touch provoking confusion
     Rekindled losses
Provide continuity
Regular meetings of
Departure

Gone defined exclamation

Cries for men's hearts to
Feel—not the punished sense of abandon
Lost, life's
     Rehabilitation seeing
Youth first
Seeing you first
Loving hope first
Renew

AGED INCOME

Fermenting agony
On the street
An old woman sits
Her hands past her knees
Holding blue tickets
Her hoping eye wanders
Will stop to buy tickets
So she'll gather
Dollars for lotto
Money her sorrows
Old age and pain
Old woman looks up
Checking her number
Winning almost
Social security
Retirement's loyalty
Her arms stretch out
In vain
Eyes drop, resume the walk

PROFESSIONAL PRIDE

Shines the science
On thick leather skin
Called mud on my hands
My silk ears, eyes
    Sense of wonder
    Fondest sleep
    And poetry
Kindling harmony

Profession's success
    Satisfactions
        Deluge
Not seeing end or
    Understanding
    Failed words
    Can't convey meaning
Poet my sins onto science
Intuitive dimensions
    File in space
Where is one molecule's
    Atomic envelope
    One's nanometer
Dry saltines
    Epi-stream

HUMANITY HEARING DEPRESSION

I cannot express what I feel in all its intensity
Crippled by the experience and rapid onset of this life
And knowing it's here and soon I'll depart
That all the while I live there
They are here
Continuing in
      And cut off—all lives

D.C. CHRISTMAS GREEN

Poor and huddled masses
On hot air vents, derelict
Chest warm in the cold
Wonder at their food, drink
And judge the use of their peril
Cheap wine and smell of urine
Forget one's plight
In suspended animation
So tightly wrapped
Rags and newspaper
Soft mattresses delivered
By carolers on the great lawn
Sung at the bar
Eyes cast from heaven
See us judge once more
As learning is lost to
Millennia moving forward
Suffering redundancy
With each day passes
As if it were less
Than our last turn around

EXOTIC WOODWORK

Trains of trucks make way
From day to day
Through that bend
And to the end
Of the trail

A tree's four hundred years
On a truck positioned
As they move to an end
Just around the bend
At the mill

A fertile valley green
Trucking tracks are seen
Along stream flanks
Ground banks sink
In the flood

Loaded truck deposits
Its woody loads in piles cut by
A jagged blade
A slice is made
In wet wood

SUBWAY AIR VENTS

Streamlined metropolis
Stone Age acropolis
Whittled wood
And sharpened stone
Concrete crevices
And exfoliated jungles
Mal-rooted minds
Upturned urns
With homeless ashes
Floating round
To tormented towns
Warm bedrooms
Dusted underground
They die

OF WATERGATE

In times of necessity
One comes to think of clarity
And often in this stream forgetting
The essence of integrity

Music, Fiction and Wrappings[11]

---

11 Most of the following poems were written while music was playing (placing myself into a mood) or while I was watching people from a distance and imagining what they were exchanging or thinking.

Silk Wrapping

Silk wrapping, planted spear
Downed dire minded, venture's gear
Denigrates, derogates
Lone unrest waits
String migrates
Snow bakes
Sore flakes
Reel in all spooled tears
High din
Slung rim
Sapient sin
Brackish butt's gin
Candor's grin, clamor's bin
Sunken sod topping plough sinks here
Silk wrapping sold passive fear

THE HEARING WAS SET ON CAPITAL STEPS

The hearing was set with what appeared to be an untested audio
system
For people not to hear
The fog was set for the sway of applause
Like the Democratic or Republican National Conventions
At election time

The background is a safe place?
No—the safe place is swayed by the rhetoric
By the applause
The queue
The hard part is to plan
What could be done
That would make a difference

Don't Confine Me

Forward step forward
Soundless beaten paper
Can't emulate rappers
Pro sonnets draw
Hardness eaten clutter
Clap deafens singers
Prose's gristle claw
Knife's cutters
Running rust
Ruins a day's brown block
Spins rumpled sculptures
Pushed off wheel's round
Sudden tape
Soundless record
Soundless food
Soundless via life
Soundless prose
Given life confines
In fad to music to beat
        To lines in pro
Pamphlets, pallets
Demon's dimensionless prose
Retained anonymously
A style bent conformity
Cause me
Course me
Train me to ignore, rescore
Refurbish, lame
Injured habits
New debits
Nun's habits
Sounds beaten
Paper caps
Warm and dear

WATCHING ANGER

Quit stomping style
Your fool's footsteps
Sewn biggest hair pile
Your lined wig-nets
Melt your ice raked
Diced smile
And whickered basket
Love mail pile

BLADED RHYTHM

A partial morning's longing
Extends through the breeze's flow
Extrudes past the moistened path
Draws on moisture
Swift sounds rebound
Clapping
All melodious tones
In bladed rhythm
As stripped coolness of
Still air comes then
Settles, erasing the tan glove
Sun bright, melting
Shadow perched on views
Launched by dreams
Whose thoughts, sweet
Sunned, awaiting night
Settling still
Sharpness dulled
And smooth-toned beauty
Rests and moves as if
Livened and still, excited
And dozing, traveling
Off with light rays
Traverse and reverse time

CURSED AND DRIFTING

Cursed with a drifting mind
That moves like a bee, a bat, a fish
From one spot to another
Though seeing anarchy
Concentration lies far away
The moon shines at night, on time
Cursed limitations
Few words come
Diction deducted
Verbally castrated
Wellspring shallow
And dry or mundane
Too many ideas
But words inane

Vacation's Club

Vacation's club
Our world
Desperate world
Discount services
Extortion ride
Sell with pride
Mistaken grace
Economic race
Sick loyal goodness
Attaches fondness
Deals, wheels
To get us spending
What role
How droll
That we use it

MISMATCHED PAIR

The woman is different from the man
The man takes what is his and asks for what is not
The woman decides what should be hers and is not
The woman gives what is hers and seeks to give what is not
The man disdains emotion, loves sex, speaks intellect, but denies affection
The woman withholds emotion, gains strain, loves sex, intellect, craves time
The woman considers emotion, affection, intellect, defining what sustenance is

Venezuela's Red-Rimmed Pool

Impressionist painting
Gauguin earth's oils
Arid raised corals
Near winter's escape
Summer's restructuring
Colors sundry
Venezuela and I
Voices from Holland
Voices from Chile
South Carolina
Texas
New Jersey
Aqua blue, green, and silver
Sparkling reflections
Agitated waters
Quiet's reflected
Aura of color
Impressionist's rainbow

Playing With Names

Dancer from New Jersey
I thought from San Jose
From Venezuela
Dance accents tell?
Nimble feet
Slender body
Youthful face
Local, I say
Nimble light dancer
Tanned, Jew Jersey

Two more dance
Quick adept
Feet move swiftly
Night's band set
Playing plaza
And what's yet
Appetites whet
Sweat, dance, twist
Dance elastic, prance

Precise, all enchanting
Silhouettes fly
All exotic sways
Neither Venezuela
Nor San Jose,
Simply New Jersey's
Dinner
All moods delight

PALM TREE BENDING

Green
Several shades
Bends
Folds
To the wind
Brown fronds
Where dying
Green where
Living
Branches burst
New shoots
From center
Leaf fronds
Tassels
Green
Woven beauteous
Palm wings toss
A non-belonging
Beach bender coconut vendor
Off sight

FLUIDTUNE

Never saw the morning fade
Gone deports
Taped sound rhythm
Drip and knock metal
Blasted, embossed by
Decades rushing downward
Flicker dreams
That heated contrast
Cast in parts played
Theaters and poets near
Killing juices of rising wisdom
Of growth
Sings feeding developed muse
Floating times wing
Winded heat
Sharpened thicker
In wound-up rushing heat
Fissure leaks lofts boarding

I WORKED HARD

I worked hard for the money
It is beautiful here
I worked hard for the money
I wish you could share
I worked hard for the money
Superficial claims
I worked hard for the money
And therefore I'm damned

FIRST MAN

There's the first man
From the mariachi band
He holds a brass trumpet
In his hand
And the second man
Holds a red rose
For the most beautiful woman
Should she pose
Within his view (second man)
For the trumpet to sing (first man)
For the evening's vigor (both men)

For song, dance, and laughter
The red rose is given
She's stunning in deed
She's holding the red rose
In her hand
In my dream, red rose in my hand
It's me and the band

EVENTS OUTRIDE

Sediments drift
Winds erode
Some arrive
Others don't
Lost on the road
Crises come
Scenario lives
The individual
Gives
Were it not for the player
Would the team win or lose?
Events, do they feed a muse?
Dance we in Brownian motion?
With canvassed thoughts
Meet destiny's reach
And
Sediments drift
Thus winds erode
In a mood

OCEAN SHALLOWS

What color are you?
Changing with the light
As clouds move over us
And waves drift by
Sometimes your blue turns green
Sometimes your coral shows
Sometimes I wonder how
Your clear blues survive at the shore

DRIFTING IN MUSIC

Do I have room for yesterday's memory?
Seems clear in temporal fog
It could have been long ago
And long from now, it will
Have been only yesterday
Forever, I see meaning determine
That I'll relax, feel blues, or rapid step
If I hear your tunes
On my wakening
Or before sleeping, trying
I'll remember without relent

At the Movie

Shadow blue
Dark brown skin
Deep Mediterranean eyes
Or is he
South American?
He woos her
Her eyes look at him
Such satisfaction
So much lover
So much desire
So much contentment
Admire
Caressing fondness
Rich coloration
Rich affection
Rich admiration
No admonitions

IT'S BEEN A LONG ONE[12]

First person:

... When I was young, I danced
On a grand stage
The audience was large
We held each other as I slid by
His hand along my waist
In the waltz, we floated on our toes
Entranced the audience
The poetry of our motion
Our art delicately portrayed
My figure was long, slender, and graceful

... When I was young, I danced
My graceful body, like a kite
Fluttered, light as a feather
I was a swan, a fairy, a queen
Forever a princess
I was all of these before audiences
And they all saw me
Gracefully dancing
When I was young, I made them cry
With my beauty
The beauty of my art, my dance

... When I was young, I danced
I was in my glory
Now I am a memory and my art
Lives in younger ones
They are me as I was once
What they were to become

---

12 The poem that follows comprises the images of two reflections interacting
about when they were "younger," comparing a first choice and justifying the
second, which was the outcome.

... When I was young I danced

Second person:

... When I was young, I strove
I had to stop my art
I left my dancing, my poetry
And my mountains behind
I made them go from me
It seemed to be the way
That is what I was told
A choice to make, must be
To give all

... When I was young, I strove
I was graceful
No one knew my face
Or the grace of my body
I studied and formed an image
Of what I was to become
Princess in a jungle
"Dancing" with my partner
A great explorer, adventure and fame
My books were open
Studying, term papers, and tests
My dreams were boundless
I would meet this man
In my classes, in the field

... When I was young, I strove
I wanted to prove
I would show my skills
They were my art
The words came slowly
The books saw me sleep
While standing, sitting
Waiting to be rescued
By the man, the hero
And no one came

... When I was young, I strove
While waiting
I became interested
And read once more
My dreams were boundless
They were endless
They never stopped
I wanted to dance in my art
My science

... When I was young, I strove
To become older
When I grew older
My body waned
Its grace and beauty left
My hope waned
But my mind grew
As I got older
More came to me
And audiences knew my work
As my art
They saw not my body
But my lips' motion
My words
They listened for my song
When I was older

... When I was young
I had not begun to live
I was growing
The slender thought's beauty
Thoughts are ageless
For me to convey
They flex and fly
Weightless ease
Slip from fantasy to force
In my hardest leaps

... When I was young
I was not destined to dance
The spirit of my hope
With my thoughts

... As I get old, I dance
Eternally on air
Fleeting wisps
Ageless thoughts shared
With those I love and cherish
Joined in common cause
Chip at the headstone
On destructive passage
Of end in time

... When I was young
I was to learn
To be born of mind
To dance with age
In eternity

WOMAN IN ORANGE

Woman in orange
Light-footed
Man in blue
Light-footed
Dance in tight rhythm
As new
Lovers would
Shiny scalp
Brunette
Dancing earlobes
Rhythm
I really love you
Love you, love you
Really love you
Really need you
Love you
Never moving
Far from holding
Dance

BLACK HANDSOME SUNSHINE

Black beauty
Handsome man
Made for sunshine
And contrasting sand
Browned companion
Seeking a sun's sent rays
Becoming darker
More exotic
Seeming remedy
Ignoring problems
Work
Love
And society
Here for repose
No surprises
Rests in eternity

BEAUTY TO THE MUSIC

Beautiful laziness
Time for thinking
Caressing my mind
Floating in an infinity
Of thought and pleasure
Earthly comfort
Sand and breeze
Shaded, combing wind
Through my hair
I know it's longer
Brown bleached
Gentle tangling
Sun soaked, saltine catch
Water soothes me
Spirit flies over meaning
In pensive moods
"Hey there!" watch me
As I disappear
Spent no energy
Into comfort's infinity
On the beach
In the shade
Sun-bright beach that
Gave me solace
In pensive great ecstasy!

ONCE OLD LOVE, LONG PASSED

You've sent your thoughts to me
Distantly
If I've felt you searching
It's me
That you touch with your
Questions
So close
While at home
The one you deny the love
She seeks
And asks
Why do you stay so far?
Even when
With you in bed holding
Your arm
Chest
At home
Just asking closer
Asking for
You
Asking for you
To see her
It's me
At home
You've forgotten
It's me

PAST FROST BITE

As the wind blows
It blows
Men gather their lines
The wind blows
Snow falls
The ground is iced
One man falls
He's covered by snow
His face exposed
Color leaves him
       Eyes icy
       Lids slowly shut
The wind blows
A friend turns back
       Quickly
Sees his dead brother
Carves the ice
Cuts blocks
Forms the shelter
For the night
The snow blows
A dead man lay there
Mists arise
He slowly breaths
Color returns
Slowly
Coming to life
As colors rush
While the wind blows

ROMANCE

Romance
No dance
What's your pleasure?
One glance
Enhance
For one another
One prance
Taken chance
Gamble your druthers
Whether finance
Presence
Lose one another

When Hearts Sear

When life sears
Gone from your soul
And tears are streaming
Down your face
Don't leave now
Don't step out now
Catch each sand grain
Slipping from your hand
Outward feelings
Glances void of emotion
As love slides past you
Can you feel me?
Clasping stretching
Reaching out to you
Blood is gone from my heart
Air is gone from this room
And I am fainting
Can you notice me falling?
Can you
Would you
Catch
Reach out to me
Childhood's innocence left me
Cold
Gone
Left me starving
Someone guide me
Though this dense
Emotional canopy
Collapse
Call me
That I might turn
Someway
Away
Catch me in the throes of
Love's dank death
That I might touch you
Before hopes dies

Intermittently Yours ...

"Intermittently yours," the letter read
But she was dead
And it was too late for the message
To touch and assuage
Passing fears of torrential losses
It seemed too late
That the love came to touch her
Finally, but too late
It's not bad
Had she stayed
And not gone

PASS LIGHT

As the sun sets
The moon rises
And we see
Daylight's now gone

I raise my head
Five times I bow
My soul is light
And yet I die

The star beckons
The earth removes
I watch a bird
Its wings flutter

I ask my love
What do you love?
And responds, "None"
"No, you"

Too young for love
The blind heart sways
One word would lie
Said: "you," meant: "I"
And none
No love
No more

SIGNING

Why call yourself but a flower's image?
Would you be real but in my vision?
Sit now in still life as I replenish
Solitude of activity, it wanes
Tilt the breeze for winds do not bend
Kiss cool air; emptiness is your man
Sit on the sea and the sand dunes follow
The life flourishes beneath me, around you
The world replenished; I sang a flavor
That prism of heaven spread its colors
And added to this life a pristine splendor
Twin moments shared
And single solitudes
Shared

UNTITLED LOVE

Carousel in a solemn prayer
Wakes the soul to despair
As it's left and leaves with all
And in its place comes love
To love
Love is love's desire
That he who loves desires
That he who loves the loved one
Loves love
That the love one feels insatiable desire
To love love and to know it
Loving someone is to reach a love
Within the whole
And the love within the whole is all
Lovers' loves and the love for all
That is, love

308

I AM BEAUTIFUL

"I am beautiful
My skin reddish brown
Come to my arms
Pale
Delicate
Waving
They're stretching out
To you
Let me touch you
Come closely as I dance
For you
Quickly as lightning strikes"

All arms clutch her shrimp
Our lady grip her prey
Lady of the ocean
Floating belle, graceful
Dancing arms
An overturned style
Iridescent our octopus sways
Wave currents, drifts
Hides to the shadow

Large, green parrotfish
Touches then
Returns again
Checking on spoils
Fleck of a trail
At the rock
Touched her sensors
She sooner returns to sight
Pulls to her chamber
Clings to captive prey
Feeds and nourishes
Digesting determinate
Any bits lost or leftover
Charm shrimp dinners
Blended with
The deep iridescent
Reddish brown cluster of
The dancer's delicate arms

DISARMING PLEASURE

Disarming pleasure
    Of good music
Distant pleasure
    When I heard it
From a yesterday, other year
    Lyrical lament
And a rhythmic grace
    Holding music
In my dream I heard
    Your song, it
Filled my soul with
    Warm elation

DANCERS TANGO

Where do loves go once they forget?
When their eyes used to gleam in anticipation, joy, and surprise
When elation showed on their lips
And emotion drew the curves of their features

Do they forget?

Why is there no gleam but a rigid acceptance?
Where is the elation when a smile is rarely out of control?
And joy not seen till gestures faintly slip the smile
Not from a lover, not me, but from a sound
Calling from a chronic channel, shop, or tuned out
Worst, seeking the mirror's smile and reflecting praise
Why don't the senses see frustration, anger's resignation
Tossed out of recovery, drowned in frustration
Left refracted all warmth, left dulled all sense
Where warmth was, do we join lost elation?
Gone animation, no joy on lips
While I look in the mirror
Dancing, epics—plausible posing

Does life forget?

GENTLY TAPPING

Quietly tapping your door
You recline there on your chair
Though I love you
See you never more
My dreams
Of what would be
Lost, rather than are
My thoughts of seeming
Rather than décor
My hopes are changing
Never more
Will I look for yesterday
With any remorse?
For times gone by
Now ever changing
And happily so lifted
A newest beginning
No, nevermore

Whispered

My pen is still going as if I've no control without
Much foreknowledge of what it will write
To me or to you
Of what it will lighten
For understanding of a kind
Unforeseen
And it comes and not too late
For its appreciation
It is coming
The movement is inherent
It does not stop
Feeling very smooth
Like music flowing across my life
A gentle melody of whispering wind

LIGHTS ROTATING

Lights rotating
Skies have set to darkness
Singing, "You loved her but you left, days gone by"
Dancers weight light rocking
Sway their hips on the floor
Soft silk pants
Soft silk dress
Rock to love gone by

Salsa-Atious

Salsa vivacious
As two proceed
One moves, placed forward
The step first stops
Stop
Moving rhythm's tides
As swimming stems
Of palms
Doused by rough wind
Step as we redraw

Now
Now
Where we are
By the fronds
Growths of palm groves
Sway wind's rhythm
Swung by breeze
Calming tropic's sand
Mango's rhythm
Reconstructs
Redesigns
Refollows me

Step, redraw all steps
Your steps
Now in palm weather
Sobriety's gone, friend
Winded moments
Garnished outside
Rhythms dance
Bells chant a cargo
And tambourine
Electronic tropics
Mango rhythm
Tropical salsa

KAREN DANCING

Karen dancing
Motherhood prancing
Light feet
Smile of passing freedom
Last night pleasures
Smile as annual passes
Future dreams
Singing memories
Tapping rhythms
Innocent pleasures
Before returning
To two small treasures

ROW FOR THE CARGOS

Row for the cargos
Henry's guitar
Ted sounds a rhythm
Jeffrey fingers the board
Rhythm in magic
All equators' rhythm
Captured emotions of
Summer heated
Neat
Weather, sand, and water
Sweating dancers

All one troupe
Sing shout
Feet slide
Magic rhythm
Wait for what may
Musicians play
Drummed guitar beats
To come
On their toes
Dancers
Two Arubans, later four
One duet in twosome

NEAR ARRIVAL

I love you well (my man)
Nothing is too great to give
And in so doing, we'll strengthen
Though if I die or am destroyed
The giver will cease to give
So that life and growth
Should not be sacrificed
Too soon, too fast
To make only your love live

DEATH'S HEART FAINTING

As she grew, love's words she kept hearing
Her life's losses drowned life's meaning
One day very soon, loneliness set in
And on one warm morning, troubles began
She thought not beforehand—was only dreaming
Mind's charm sent her heart screaming
For help and protection, no one would give her
She died the next morning, no one to look after
A pitiful waste of a kind heart fainting
Into the loneliness, lost in the painting
She met death and left all crying

FIREFLY

The firefly would dance
In the night, the entrance
She catches him with her glance
And shortly thereafter, romance
A firefly was in my room last night
And its light shown on the wall
It hopped sporadically in its flight
And flickered with its call

Between life and death this is the margin
And for the good, there's the pardon
To all truth seekers' humanity
There's the loved one

The firefly dances again
In the solitude of my room
This she does in quiet refrain
A light to my spirit, my moon

Sulking Solitude

I'm listening to your music
Soft and ethereal
My soul sways gracefully
I feel it with the music
Leave me not alone

I walk along the shore
The song I am singing
Is in remembrance of you
Call my name
And I will come

Footsteps are nearing
Closer they resound
Cry out my soul
I tremble in the darkness
God, hold up my head!

Crashing; they crush me
These mighty battalions
That march in the night
Cleanse me as I die
Peacefully then, I go

DREAMING LOVE

Could one's crush understand?
The feeling when two touch hands
A feeling
A decorative frame yet, clearly one-sided
One's heart's smile is quickly subsided
It's quick
One way
Lost message relay

Logic's consoles rapidly lost it
One hand drowns in compulsive fidget
Life's dealing
Independent souls can't bliss one way
Sole-authored fallacy wrought decay
It's wilt
One's sway
Lost desire, dismay

WATCHING A QUARREL AND REVERSE

Nerves pinched, festered eating
Bound and knotted soul's moraine
Thinking at all gives queasy feelings
Dumfounded hope, hunger's replay
Distress inclined, pitch increasing
Falls down premise, come days

Done ordeals, care's heart peeling
Crying stomach bent on decay
Squelched aspirations, found stealing
Leaving emptiness in drive's wake
Wanting hopes back, confidence chasing
Counted memories forced their place

Every ear caught voices speaking
Cacophonous groans attest
Grueling, lost hours fighting
Dreaming whispers, hearts inquest
Cemented minds, thoughts redacting
Recounted times, one refurbished test

A reverse

Love cuts passes, death's hold relenting
Resuscitates, exhumes a dormant Oz
Chalks and dissects, thoughts on healing
Hung apparitions dissolve, time's saws
Cut 'cross rigid boards—traps dissolving
Emergent elations, reflections pause

Joy, once refreshed, excites living
Self-attest esteem's respect
Contest and rescind all demeaning
Seems to disperse and forget
Hate's once erosive ferment thriving
Now found, loving heart's infect
A trust that, shared among us,
      Has a lasting and unqualified meaning

LISTENING TO LOVE'S AND LIFE'S TUNES

The intensity of their duet
Drew my ears
A singularity in art
That swept and held captive
All emotion
That response could not free
From the stronghold
Unbalanced gravity
Their despair communicated
Fills some souls
Split by times departing
Separating destinies
In which any die
Beauty in this falling
Without heart's promise
As angels fly
Despite the hold
Of humans once grasping
A single moment when
They were one

Wine Listening to Music

I've begun dreaming
Of odd things, you know
Memories of the past sifting
Into my thoughts, go slowly

Give me your love
Your touch, loving, and warmth
Affection you cannot rob
From the gifts that from you glow
Lest I dream of the other times
Fantasy and frustration twining
Into each other to sound the chimes
Of my world creating

Don't let me down or even level off
Don't let me out or keep me cold
Distance and not touch are too rough
For my sensitive soul

Romance me, love me, need me
Don't make me feel misfit
Hold my heart in your clasp
And don't let me go

WAR'S ARCHWAY: DEAD SOLDIER SINGS

Arched
Marches
Rose wine
"You corrected
I remember
That once
Love, memories
Hear echoes
Distant drums approaching
Sounds familiar
Consume a tune
Buffered
Seeming dull
Soil and grass beds say
I'm away

"Cask arched
Meets the ground
Words hum
Drums roll
A coronet sounds
Our moments surrender
All passed times
Perches where we'd sit
Then
Where we'd dream
Planning
Tripped tunes
Fleeted
Left here"

Arched swords
Reverence
Barely breathed
Moments erode
Consume
Time's accelerants
Fallen sides

Drop silence
Iridescent dreams
Once ours
Drop life
As arched swords do
Touch ground
And anchor death
A soldier's breath

"Arched arbors
Waited
Near me
All parts
Suggesting
My soul was home
When in fact I'd gone"

Correcting sounds
Drums roll
Mark synchrony
Your face wordless
At your door

Arched gate
White stone
Feet sedated fill
A ceremonial frame
My grave
Kept clean
Named my name
Green carpets
Ground's grass
Resurfaced
With time, silence
Stones recline
Graveyard fragments

Hosted arches
Whitewashed
A name worn stone
Part buried
Moss greens

Fern fronds
Shower flower beds
With spores
Birthed fresh meadows
Kept some meaning
From a wake
Long after
Our deaths' times

Flags arched
Softened breeze
Fogs roll in
A lone coronet
My sound
Relives memories
Sounds pass
The arches large
Encircled
Solitary plaque
My ground

Arched
Bent
Over graves'
Spelled names
Etched and worn
Stones reverence
An ambient peace
Settling times for
Life's departure and
Love's languish
All confluent memories
Enter eye margins
Finding a balance
Resting silent
And wait—I wait
For our coronet sounds
Once again
That will
This time, I hope
Mark a peace—

BETROTHED, OFF-CENTER

It wasn't long ago, reminded of a time
We loved one another fonder than today
Our song's first hour had barely rung its chime

Something cut warmth away
Lost the love that clutched our hearts
Our souls drifted, passing each other
Outwardly with visibility poor

Time sent our faces' good-bye gestures
To use, when would turn
Back-to-back, with eye whites stale
Pressing forward, preparing
Blindly, the stare ... shot-off fairly?
Both minds gone
Our hearts, equally impaled

BURIED LIGHT

Dark eyes
Long eyelashes
A serious look
Deceive despair

Masked brilliance wherein lies
Complexions fair and pensive
Each, competitive spirits soften to waves
Light, magnetic, temperature, sound, all
Forming a gentleness of distant console
Insulated lies a willingness of heart
Every inch of body stands with its mask
Between two intended embracing arms
Controlling exclamations

Abandons love's exposure
Silent strapped it stays
Sending no speech
Bars description
Cold insulation
Advertisement and scene

Deeper, discrete
Sanctum holds marvel
Definition sets encrypted
Awaiting translation, excavation
By life's esteem

Can time kill the woman's love for life
My God, how did our life survive?
So meant to join and make the best of it?
Instead they join for strife

Love is not turmoil
Love is not distrust
Love is not duality
Or tied cruelty
It must unite in fervor

Two who would meet?
Sharing anxiety together
Rather one turmoil than apart?
Taken separate, breathed expanse
Directing honest comfort
While looking to reunite
Head to the other side?

"Good-bye" indeed hard
Inflicted severe, pain, yours or mine
On their own die, each sense
Occasions demolished
No clear instruction
Uncertain outcome, can ...
Unfortunate to be in love
Wrong time, places
Neither you nor I are bad

Time's current slice through love
I wish I could not feel, capped
By greed determination
All is circled dreaming, unreal

Fever's gripped listless time
Why hard to overcome?
A path's demise, not the people
Letting go, peace not craft
"Break a wick, but not its candle"

Still sorrow rides only
They say, "For a while"

Beasts and Child's Play

FREEZE!

Freeze, freeze, freeze, freeze, freeze!
This ass is cold!
As to venture as has been told
Of heroic humans yon heroic deeds
In such dispersion of precious heat

Freeze, freeze my soul, my ass is cold!
Keep heaters on
I will not live to meet the dusk
Or pass the dawn of morning white splendors
Of snow powdered meadows
Help, I'm cold!
Let the warmth draw near!
Sun appear!
It's cold in here!

Little Horrors Bite Me

Eaten by mosquitoes
Tonight
All nights I donate my blood
Insect evolution
Donation
Swearing each time
To self-comfort
Closed walls
Refuges from proboscid guns
Isolated stalked faces
Tap-tap type-bitten holes
Punctured skin
Dilute unclotted juice
Delicate gut knives
My pierced essence
       Lost—to fiendish hives

Mosquito's Bar-B-Q

Rapacious appetites
Fiendish winged pirates
Red jewels one by one
Sucked life from
Rich, pulsating veins
From life's flow they take
Cell by cell in liquid masses
Never stopping to say thanks
Those parasitic little wrasses
Gone blood type A
Rh+ to be purged
From deceased red cells
By guts too small to care
Too quick to digest
All, little nightmares
My helping them
Forced past selection
Top new generations
Careful evolution
Giving usually
Without demise
Care wise

PLANET ZERON

"We are from planet Zeron"
"Planet Zeron?
We know this
We see you talk of conquering
        Advertisements
You've been told
You're overtaken
Do you refuse?
The standing as you bow
        To purchase me
Drink"

You look at me
Spoon drops, you frown
I smile pleasantly

You don't see; my worlds apart
I do not feel you searching
The moment parts
You are removed
From my reality
You're gone
I see you and wonder now
What begets ephemeral clouds?

Ephemeral
Streams and Pits

Summer Stop

Proud spindles of golden grass
Reach for the sun to touch
In the drying summer last
Until autumn's crushed
Bread of life
From golden hills
Penetrating strife
Grow freely, to your wills

Frustrated Moments

If only I had a poets genius and a God-like inspiration
I would beg my soul and task my talent to deliver
Phrases, real communications of what my soul knows
Those moments that it only knows but should not only feel
To share and well would be the exact communication:
A perfect reward and utmost pleasure!

PROFESSION'S COSTS AND BALANCES

The freedom to write and research
To teach, live, sleep, and think
What would it be if all this were gone?
Invisibility buys freedom
Low budget buys direction
So that presence is not pertinent
But products are boundless
Freedom makes them
Despite paper distraction
Evaluations cut quality from production
Since evaluations seek production
Trend marks obsolescence

Separated

Kindness is but a gesture's glance
Reminding me of our last dance
When we flew and soared over castles and streams
When our spirits kidnapped us on our dreams
We shared the laughter, song, and sorrow
And, holding hands, promised each other tomorrow
Here we are now on vacation's start
Not holding hands, not being together
Not moving along as three in the weather
But withering we are as if one trip
And singing silent, as our tongues move and trip
You love; you want each other, not me
Come take me, us—you, family
Let's all meet

THE OTHER SIDE

Sweltering smog falling on the whimper of crushed steeples
Once endeavored to deify open skies
The layered domain that neither God nor world want
Stays stagnant, a pool filling with silt and eutrophic water

In the Dumps

Should I go on a pilgrimage as men have?
Shave my head and let hair grow
Wear black, abstaining from sin?

Would one month of sacrifice
Make you come back to me
As you did on Madison Street
When you and I first met

You since sought quiet's sound
Left our hearts pained, wondering
Your aim, your direction now

For what? For why?
You leave us dry

CEASE LONELY TIMES

To cease lonely times
To cease broken hearts
To cease broken truths
Among them promises, oaths
And sworn love
How will it swear again?

MOONLIGHT

Why can't the moon lighten the room?
The empty sound when you're not here
When come the moments I feel alone
My thoughts pull you to me
When your thoughts rest and you are lonely
You call me to you
When there's such a moment and you're not near me
Little seems clear to me
The stars are the only light
Even with a fully lit moon

PLEASE, CAN I FEEL?

Please, can I feel warmth and affection again?
Contours that are gentle
Warmth enters deeply
To depths where I've despaired
Smile and kindness enthuse
My heart to hope
Is it there or just more
Impossibility?

Dulled Blades Rip Me

Here
Every time I eat
I see wealth
Every time I'm tempted
The contrast
Cuts across me like
Coarse, dulled blades
Ripping within me
There must be a way to
What makes the difference?
Now
What to give up?
Willing to share?
Such differences now
Dulling blades
Further worn
By the weather
Motivations and ideals
Tongues tied

REALITIES SET IN TOO SOON

Sometimes realities set in too soon
I've often wondered how to dull the senses that see them
Disjoined geographic and emotional both similar
Stops between joining
As fate would seem to always want it
There seem to be real curses and redundant losses
Often counted before they occur
Still, intuition called them correctly
This too?

Raised for another planet or another time
Gone in this one
And enough still for a time not yet come
How can one set out for goals?
Knowing full well that they are destroyed by seeking

The wind sweeps through, taking all my memory
Of how-to and of lessons, such painful ones
What to do next?

YOU SEEMED

You seemed large and generous
Your strength caught me at my weakest time
My hope, despair, love, pain fused
Moments needed holding
Tall and strong
My arms reached
Holding only wanting but tore away
Not engulf and not smother
I ache so much

Some Didn't Last

Why then do you ignore me?
Why must I rest?
From emotional turmoil
We cannot divest
While willing we love
One another for life
It seems we can't avoid the spurious strife

Changing Tunes, Morning Is Saturday

This morning is Saturday
But the night, endless, continues
I listen to musical tragedy
Sink deeply into the view
Dirge-like tune pops all balloons and
I see my own play

Over, over, and more
Pounds a drained brain
Funneled into anti-cathartic wonder
This is not to feel sorry
So much as to ask
Forget today, when does tomorrow begin?

In centered self demise
Haunting emptiness
Sounds of life seem beyond
Limits of audible senses
I can't hear tenses
So I try to clear my eyes

Hoping dust settles in a mind imploded
Lashes close over my shut eyes
Torn, depression's garment falling
My flesh melts and rusts iron
Feeling robbed of my strength
What motion bones possess is all mired

The holding broke
All fresh heart vessels
Deoxygenated, hyperventilated
Long enough
So that nourishment ceased
To feed a depressing mind

Then CDs switch over to upbeat tunes
I toss and shift a pillow
Move blankets back
Then roll over
The pain and doom—all finally gone

OLD LETTER'S SULTRY LINES

Sultry lines
Conveys no small lie
Adultery sorry
May never arrive
Or deny from envy
What never is tried?
To sway from needy
Attempt for your eye

Laid back
My back
Feel my pleasure
Hold back
Catch flack
You've lost the treasure

Too Slow

I feel as though the day ends too soon
The sunset is abrupt
Dawn comes to pass before my eyes open
And all that goes slowly, leads
Dragging my progress

In my progress, I go slowly
In day's work, I meander only
Wishing for a step that brings me steeply
To a new step more than the last lowly one

Once Hit Bottom

What does one say to a sickened heart
That cannot pour forth words of melody?
Why has the inspiration vanished and hope dulled so
You thought he cared
That he loved you
And you returned love in the way you knew, with affection
It was strange and foreign, this honest warmth
And gentle kindness
"Toss it aside; it's repulsive," I hear
Please help me, I feel so despaired
I've no one to talk to, no friend but you
What happens when you want something so badly?
Do everything you can to get it
But destroy your clear vision and ruin your goal
All with anxiety
And then how to break free
Of something you want to hold on to
It will not change
You are not powerful enough to change it
So these ups and mostly downs
Will continue
With little relief of this torture
Till you wish you were part of the plant life
Help me find my peace
Help me understand
I do not want to hurt
I do not want to be hurt
I am tired of it
Why has he given up?
Why won't he try?
When someone you love is dying
You die also
Please let us live
In peace
With warmth
Kindness understanding
And let our minds commune
If this is not to be
Then please at least remove the agony

My words are limited and
I cannot write all I wish here
But understand and help me
Tomorrow I'll awake
It will be just as bad
It's been this way for months now
Where I sleep only to escape
My conscious memories hoping
That my dreams will bring
Some fantasy of happiness
That I may remember
The past and look forward to the future
Unconsciously

Accepting Lies

I thought he loved me; he did not
He did not know how to nor wanted to know me
But fantasized of what he thought he felt
He shares himself with another
But claims he does not
And yet how can my eyes deceive me
That what they see is "no"
Disconnected, non-recognition
I'm the fool to suffer so willingly
For anyone cursed decay
Then, if not love, say so!
Why can't I say, "Go"

ESTEEM'S ANGER

Is love so close to hate, to fear?
A glass of wine has such magic in it
It dulls the senses and the brain
I wish it would my memory too
Why was I born into this notion of world?
So ill-equipped or so self-pitied
Keep your fracas
Keep your art
Do I demand so much?
That you be loyal, honest, and not cruel
Why do you maim my heart
So willingly, indifferently?

Willow's Heart

Crying to return, tall oaks oversee
My head bent low

I don't see the silhouette of
The proud barn owl passing
Nor hear the territorial song of
The yellow meadow lark singing

Today I feel empty
Sunk in a cave's deep darkness
Where even bats don't roost
On the coldest of lonely days

I sit at a fresh stream
A willow weeping
Leaves tapping the graveled sand
Where my tears fall

The weeping willow tree
Is very much like me
It mourns in the sun
Bends over, limbs dropping
While growing
Strongly treasured
In all hearts except its own

SOLUTIONS

The solution to frustration is in the womb
The solution to desolation is in the tomb
The solution to jealousy is to wound
The destruction of love is fear's harpoon

This womb is lost, frustrations kill
The tombs contain dissolved will
Jealous wounds, fear instill
Biased survival's love is nil

    Then

        Wrenches teach
        Violence deep
        Grave remorse
        Void ruins
Loss fills

Act's Frustration

What he felt
So far censored
Throb—heart pulses
Indecently moved
The turned-on pleasure
Of any inner feeling
All left to hang
Without destiny

Set to accept
Determined to accept
Those remembrances
Ones longer
Than love unexpanded
Short memories
Of gentle triumphs
Seen passage to travel

Not without emotion
Once became certain
His life's trail
All trained suppression
Dwarfed expressions
Remaining, remembering
Remaining conscious
Ignorant of silence distanced
Eroded secure feelings
Of rights to be in love
No matter how bad a script
The romantics sing of love
And thrive on the beauty of its song

EMPTY SHELL

Clouds shift faster than can be counted
Rain seeps through
Its waters stagnant
Withering winter denies spring
And any pleasure that streams
Holding only frustrations
The moisture in the eyes of those who cry
Into a day's self-denial

THOUGHTS ENVISION

I wonder what at times invades
Shades of brightness within us
Stings and perpetuates gloom
That rests about our souls
Then transform

Reaching for a piercing light or heat
To redress clouds into sunshine
Letting airs of possibility string from despair
Hope's creative mold in our hands breathes
Secrets while hidden atrophy
Losing their functions
Consciousness free, envisions beauty

An originality of imagination
Makes life's gait emerge with strength
Strides gain, outrun, and toss the burdens
Cast by weighted and demonic shadows

BIDDING MESSAGE

Mail
Male
Uttering
"I've been gone"
Try—anger back
A vengeful sack
    To sink
    String the noose
    Not loose
Fit to slip
    Tightly
    'Round
    Limp neck
The payment
    Mass disorder
    Greeted anger
    Blank gaze
Wonder and question
Saying ... "A change of pace!"

Euphoric[13]

---

13 My thoughts and love are dedicated to the federal and state parks, province parks, and biosphere reserves of the United States and Canada—their interpreters, managers, curators, scientists, volunteers, and administrations all put their bodies, professionalism, ideals, and ethics on the line, sometimes with considerable personal cost.

LIFE FROM DEADMAN CANYON

When you are at school
Or at work
And when life's purpose
Seems to fail you
Recall mountain streams
Flowing timelessly over granite beds
Recall green meadows
Purple, yellow, violet, mauve
Red
Tints of life
Can you fortune ever be greater
Than these recollections
Experiences approaching
With cool waters sifting through
Glaciers and soft peat litter
Here is the home of poetry, love, and generosity
What more can one desire but to share
And to possess those memories
With the hopes of returning?
They come to me
Repeatedly
On demand, gratefully

VERMONT MEADOWS

We are free at breakfast, walking
Lazy, rusted, and wanting more
Harmony of a tractor's distant grind
Clear sound of a near song's meadow
Not knowing who to thank for it

Brilliant rays, dew on the grasses
Keep me poised in rememberment
Those who can't share
This delight and bewilderment
Crisp valley meadow's wallow

Rocky Main Shore, Monday Break

Child of Monday
Feel the Maine breeze
Seashore a rocky intertidal
See the gull snatch its prey
Aloof, I wander, and foam melts round me
Pebbles tumble, and granite glistens
Beneath the stir of water's motion
The rocks sulk into the ocean
Their shoulders lifted by the sky
Yellow warblers sing your song
And let me see what I long for
The road is long time
Sees no waste
Push on to new country
Even wilder and more untamed
Not tinted by industry
No disruption in its domain

UNDERWATER

Underwater sea
Luscious composite
Earth's library
Past history
In glass like sound
Coral reef colors
And elk horn sculpture
Blacks, yellows, blue, magenta, and purple hues
Singling out movements
Mobile purposed adornments
Corral stag horn
Brain deposits
Squid and parrotfish graze
My body floats
From earthly attachments
To other dimensions
Beauty in vision
In all directions
Generation's wonders
Evolution more
Change produces
Such heavenly shores

Azure Blue

Azure blue
And yellow maize
Yellow maize
On your young contour
Mine is bulging
And slightly faded
Black shadow
And azure
Azure blue
Of coral waters
Makes us all
Same age really
Infinity
Life's time I see
Gripping as we grow
Time that strips us
Of baggage
And form
Light's contour
Skin unfolded
Making secure
Remains, thoughts, and
Demure azure water
Saltine sea, life, and reckoning

Room Is Dinner

Moon is dinner
Pile of wood drift
Sea drift
Ear on a conch shell
Song is smooth
Mellow
Shuffle, fresh
Ankles and knees
As waists bend
Hips beat
Bodies undulate
Push sea drifts
Saltine wok and seashell
Wooden table
Musician's spell

TWILIGHT

Crashing over rocks
    Sound is muffled in foam
Sand is white
    Sifted by the water

Fresh mists sift
    Cleansing moisture
Salted residues
    Coat my skin

A rock-lined shore
    Sifts with separate tides
Limits of sand
    Stand beyond
To stretch my sight
    Through clean water
Strands of small pools
    Rock the tide
Boulders beneath give
    Fresh steam

Clear air
    Fills my lungs
Each breath is caught
    Cooled and
Condensed to haze
    Blending
Invisibly melting
    Into coastal fog

Beneath
    This sun
Storm clouds strew
    To paint a horizon
I'm left
    Entranced
Earth's glimmering star
    Sinks and sends
A flashing light
    My irises close

The sun has now set
    And travels
Waters crash
    Mists are rainbows
I recline, rewind
    And wait
Tomorrow's sound
    Enhanced by light

NEW DAY

Trees bend; branches arc
Lights dim; sight meets dark
I sleep by; night marks
Day makes entry; as next day
Cycles recur; recycle, replay
Eternity rewinds: life's recast

Retrospect Belize

Intertidal retrospect
All point adventure
Circumspect
Convey motion
Soft and still photos
Lively eclectic
Coastal coral shore
Blue
Water and
Green-ribboned fruit
Angels dance
'Round anemones
Stars, abalones
Low tide's romance

FOR THE WOLF

Moon crosses the sky
Wolf cries
Where are her babes?
She cries again
A sound on hallowed ground
For life

Remember its echo
When you've grown
And called your young
And found them fled also
Gone with their mates
Where the wolf went
Dead
Where the coyote and the lions go
And won't return

So when you see no wolf sign
Search farther and dread
Lest it be no children's song
That you cry for
Remembering, grieving
When their days began
And times ended

Day is now night
Where our children stood
And no one sorrows about this rare land
Or about them
That freedom meant more
Than for just the man

CALIFORNIA NOMADIC HILLS

The hills are golden
And roll as far as the eye can see
Meadowlarks fly from them
And their songs surround me

Stacks of hay on wayward diesels
Wide snaking aqueduct winds
Sideline pavement's cars roam
Wind towers' long arms churn

Atmosphere's been pushing
Nomads' sloped barriers forward
All turning slowly, shift, slide
Stack to form the hardened sand

Slopes forever lining beaches
Forever on a continent's crust
Wandering, splitting, eroding
In deluges of arms, cars, and hard rains

SQUID, I LOVE YOU

Spotted white on dark
White dorsal stripe
Spots come and go, changing
Color dark elk horn coral
To pink translucent flesh
Two swim together
Watchful eyes
Undulating elegance
Dynamic color
As they analyze frames
Made of the sea, spirits
Gifts of the ocean
Life looks out
Clear eyes
Organized curiosity
Penetrating stares
As we watch one another
Focus keenly
Ethereal calm
Ethereal inspiration
Angels of the sea
Awesome elegance
Beauties excel over all

SIERRA

Take me to a mountain of jagged terrain
Much like the Sierra Nevada mountain range
White and black grano-diorite
Green and blue mountain meadow and morning due
To leave is like leaving home
Take me to what the mountain gives
Then you will have given heaven
To a homeless, lost immortal
Take me to a glacier or a high alpine meadow
To satisfy my craving

HOPE

I often think
　　Of those moments we've had together
My Sierra peak
Your silent strength breathes
Makes the way for my inspiration
Strength
Vitality
Mountaintop
Beauteous array
Now from far, I recollect
You know of where I speak
Why can't this heaven catch me?
Share your serenity
No strife-ridden worlds, your peak's cap
Take me back to that world
Let my happiness unfurl—uncontrolled, unshielded
And in full embodiment of my soul
Before death takes its toll

SHASTA

Nature is showing me her album
Portraits of green and brown
Skies of bright blue and lakes of aqua
Manzanita bows to an oak
And the oak to a fir
The fir to a pine
And a bird flies over them

It's Shasta, here, they say
Water makes its way
Spreading itself over a winding valley
As a snake, it moves
Through the pines
Over red sand beaches
And the echo of a sun's radiance
Reverberates on the walls
Above wooded canyons

HELEN'S ASH

Like an untraced beauty
Its head blown off
Still standing and proud
Devoid of blemish
To the virgin beauty
Nature's innocence
Lost demise
Only a top
Small part
Total's fragment
Grey expense
New lava dust
Thrown, tossed
Spread fresh spar
Forests hewn
Toppled water weight
Under foot of God
When earth sneezed
Strew forth its blood
Cacophonous "Achoo!"
Saint Helen's crown flew
Cones burnt bursting
Seed green grass carpets
Tomorrow's year
Over buddies buried
Log, graze, and deer
Past underlay
The massive weight
Lustrate mountain
St. Helen's cheered
Spring's dew

WHY DOESN'T THE RIVER SLOW?

Why doesn't the river slow its course after the storm?
Rock's refugia bring only hopeless rescues from later deaths
By drowning
Rains nourish and withdraw the breath of vegetation
Rotted
Cleansing, the earth cries as old makes way for the new
And summer's desiccation
First flowers aren't stirred by the news
Daffodils
They flower and assert the signal is clear, was present
Was significant to them
Spring is clear

INDIA'S FOREST LANGURS STIR - 1

Light saltates
Branches vibrate
Sting consciousness
Feeling stir
Warm fur
Of feeling deliciousness
Cry alone
Rejoice reborn
To another inspiration
Hey, see
Respite and glee
From my rapaciousness
Forgive
Sullen madness
From stress
That comes relentless
Let hope
Nature's brought
The constant inventiveness

Langurs Stir - 2

Lights saltate
Branches vibrate
Sounds awake from motionless

Feelings stir
Old langur's fur
Fingers scratch, all relentless

Stretched out strait
Broad armpits wait
Beg for help out of madness

Hands come home
A "fine-toothed comb"
Tips pinch—all's meticulous!
Groom

Back arch rolls
Each comfort grows
Groomer doused all restlessness
Groomed one lies
Motionless
Resting

MOSQUITO PIERCING KISSES

There are so many spots
On my skin
That I can't begin to count them
They all align
With my wrists' designs
Arms, ankles, face, and dressings

Artists speckle
On neck and face
My hands and nose's arbor
The hungry evening
      solicitor-esses
Buzz about all human hosts
In all streets' lit light posts

To sup on Danish smorgasbords
Focus on which spot
First feed
Without concerns as to malaria
They donate thinners to bleed me
Dry

Beauty's Shadows

Imagine moving through
Three or four forest types
Imagine first thinly wooded savannah
In which deer wander, spotted deer
Then as woods get thicker, the Sambar come
Followed by Asian bison, by elephants
Denser still as woods close in
Giant squirrels
Langurs move into our forest
Making me feel so small
In their graceful leaps and swings
Moving among old canopy tops, down
To younger saplings
Elephants come
Wild boar and a few macaques
Tiger's missing today from this part
Of the Western Ghats
It's away from our interruptions
Recluse where it hunts
Only occasional shadows pass
Beside tigers' grassed wet openings
Fruit bats swift
Passing dreams and hint movement
In stream's shallow moorings

CORAL EYES

Look up closely at the
Coral eyes
The reef would look at you
Coral eyes
Miniscule tentacles around
Coral eyes
Millions in limestone
Coral eyes
Basslets, parrotfish, angels all surround
Coral eyes
Could a master paint the reef and
Coral eyes
Observing the deep and watching with
Coral eyes
How nature's wonder of the reef
Is monitored by
Coral eyes
When we look for life beneath
Coral eyes
It's sad that most miss the
Coral eyes

LOST FIRE STAGE

Fires scar the golden home
To chalk from beaming meadow
Churns coal and meets the sun
By hand of fate turned ash-laden

Rain

Don't go away
   Dear storm
   Dear weather
We need your rain
Ten miles northern
Join us southward
Let your flash
Send us the rain

I see the streaks
Of yellow dirt grey
And time's measures
On the traveling sphere
Beneath clouded platforms

California tropical winds
Dry summer droughts
A dry load, water's blight
Desperate, I'm wishing truly
For a summer rain

GOBBLE-GOBBLE

Turkeys gobble
To lightning bolts
To thunder's pace
The orchestrated sounds
Of gobbled birds
And dog barks
Measure rhythms for
The whiplash of branches
And crackling fire

BEDROOM'S WINDOW

You sleep soundly
Rolled over in comfort
And as I lay wakened
Foxes singing
Gazing at the pyramid snow crest

All beauty

Soft sounds of melodic rain
Catch thoughts and transport
My own dreams found
Fondest memories shared

A grace's ocean waves
Sounds shift into
Sweeping winds
Rivers rush
Falls, "Timber!"
Down cut canyons
Where the earth moves

Glacial crusts cut
Moraine-filling sketches
Landscapes of alpine meadow
Awake and wakened dreams
Lift a sleeping body's soul
Free of motion catch

The morning's conception
Birth of the last winter stars
As heightened blues reveal
Snow caps webbed
Lay over granite greys

Science Institute's Garden[14]

This is the tree where the fruit bats come to feed
Birds of night fly gracefully under stars
Sweep down, low upon the dark, watch
There on the corner administrative walk
Close to building's open, sandy walkways
Bougainvilleas turned grey in night's color
Moon or moonless nights to home
To feed on fruit trees
Imposing and watching, awaiting dusk
Animate and fill, fold
Surrender to blend
With the night's tree bark
Foraging among sounds and shadows
In Bangalore

---

14 My stay at the Indian Institute of Science in Bangalore and interactions with
   its fine students, staff, and scientists was an inspirational time, scientifically,
   culturally, and poetically.

IDAHO'S ARROWHEAD

A white-flanked arrowhead
On the Sawtooth's crest
Juts into blue clouded skies
Sharp black ridges
Dip rock-sharp to alpine meadows
Wooded hills dip into soft moss
Where moons rise in summer
Where we see Idaho's ghost riders
Soar, bursting in orange glow
Out of the regal snow-capped tower

THOMPSON'S HILL

Summer's dried white wheel drags
Trimmed spent hay, fractured bent boards
All pivot 'round rust iron seam's welding
Fallen nest twigs, flown breezes, and immigrant colds
Flush, in tandem, flow southward

Parachute spiders, obscure, waft, miniscule
Gyrate, lost in an all-magnetic migration
Hawks, swifts, geese meet cloud bursts
While small parachutes set, hydrate
Setting somewhere near but southward

Gastric leaves, dried red berries
Douse brown grasslands
Acorns darken ground sod templates
Aged oaks' roots encircle, hardened
One branch rubs, cracks, fallen, crushes
Dye's bleached shale's chromium luster
With sounds, buff-split layered rocks

Warmed springs' hazed fogs
Cut crystalline ice laces
Spray soil's nested fruiting mosses

Sierra spires grow a hooded green
With red buds, emergent limbs amidst
Small hooded collars
Red iridescent sheens
All peer-referenced hummer's wings dive
Chase met rivals' charted displays

Birth blankets, perch on sill basket nests
Tucked in angles of budded maple arches
Lightly resting songs and dreams
Softening fractured diction's words
Into life's tender verbs
Clothing on a song's formed wheel

VEINS IN THE LEAF

I hold in my hand a leaf
Its tissue pliant and green
Five major veins address its length
And the reddest one makes the point

ACACIA LEAVES

I'll not forget looking up at the sky at night
Through the fine lace spun by the acacia leaves
Against the grey of post dusk

I'll not forget the frugivorous bats
Coming each evening to their forest
Regular trees to feed and roost, so huge
Then there was that giant squirrel
As if from another time
With tufts on its ears
And contrasts of dark
All reddish brown and beige
Stately and big enough to make
One wonders which geological plate
And era it came from

BREATH OF SPRING

The star begins to shine
Emerged
Blending years' springs
Summed, into unity

Rising on snow's once-carpeted hills
Shimmering splendors
Evened slopes of recent melt
Dowse color on meadows

The grass's infusions of fresh green
Fold and twine, turn, open
Toward the rays of the dazzling sun
Emergent flowers of carpeted hills

FIREPLACE

A fire burns, and its heat caresses me gently
Sleeping, breathing, the cat purrs on my legs
The music floats in the room
Voices are distant sounding, a tree falls
Ashes burn
The room is empty

Glaciers' Dawn Lilies

It seems like it's getting cold up in the mountains
Fall is taking the way from spring and the bird's songs are no
longer heard
The sun sets much earlier now, at least before dinner
Trees are rapidly dropping their leaves for strong brushes of
street sweepers
I wonder what happened to the warm days
Where meadows were painted with blossoms
And granite glaciers were still frozen, their lips lined with fawn
lilies
The branches are naked and have no protection from the rain
The clouds are motionless, yet melt over the earth in the darkest
haze
The animals have deserted us and left for southern warmth
And we have deserted our friends for the security of electric
heat

MORNING SOUNDS IN THE GHATS[15]

Morning under moonlight
And disappearing stars
Rumbles of trucks and carts
Create the morning hum
Soft silhouettes and clear images
A single column of ants crawls by

Parakeets flying overhead
Chirping melodies, birds mooring
Join feeding sites at breakfast
Men gather quickly with teacups

Almost one per door
Sounds knock to wake
Gently, "knock, knock, Knock, coffee, coffee"
I hear "coffee," stir from dreams

In the background shuffles tunes
Chuckles and laughter
From outside burned fire
That jovially greets morning

A house crow calls
Joined by a breakfast crew
No sooner car's engine barks
Smiles all join, "Wonderful to greet you!"

At these chipper times, with hot tea
Warm bread and pastries
In a dark forest camping
That I sit, relaxed, and watch all the ants crawl by

---

15 Southern Ghat Mountains of India

CONSTELLATIONS ON THE DECK

It's a myriad of constellations
Of efforts and wages
Synchronized dances
Speaking in time
Frolicking dragonflies
Lake top reflections
Of May's satin moon
I feel silk drawn
From cocoons unraided
Incense burns strong
Walloping flight
Fluffed fresh feathers
And bread from heaven
Dangling onlookers set by
Red orchids' blossoms
Dressing generations
Earthen young
Raven hoards
Swept doorsteps
Crowd together, looking on
Remain forever
Commonness sharing
Rhapsodies born

Religious and Philosophical[16]

---

16 I often rely on a context of religion to express emotions of anger, sympathy, regret, and more. These expressions don't come frequently, but they all come when I've been moved and feel somewhat wordless. Then I'll rely on music to help me figure out what sounds are coming out of my head. Also, a while ago, at a French grammar school where I was sent to keep up my first language, French, the students attended regular masses a few times a week. The catholic services were in Latin. None of us knew or learned Latin; we only had to pronounce it correctly. As with the Danish services at my parents' church, I would lose myself in the music, watch people sing, and absorb their expressions and chants. I would fabricate my own words, "thinking" them along with the congregation. Certain classical pieces, chants, blues, and gospel music bring out a hum to my mind that transfers its sound to my pen in the form of words. In all honesty, the meanings of the words don't enter into what's written so much; it's the flow of the sound through my ears or mind.

SUNG

Slated for a Sunday's mass and prayer
Sultry hot sun, rendering sympathies
Young voices carry to tomorrow's gait
In hunger await all outstretched arms
Ill-gotten pleasure wastes through dawn
Upon a morrows sunrise and soft-spoken dew
To whisper emotion, it can carry yonder
Bated for Clementine, times aware
Sensing tomorrow's seer and share

SONGS OF MIRRORS

Clear specter mirrors and casting devotions
Seeming might crumbles in air
Plenty remarks at her loss of invention
And desperately alights in dull detention
      to hide
Let me guide and lift your heart
Let me wrap your sorrow, loneliness
Caught in harping triumph of battle
In ways which differ from your instruction
I'll carry your soul to sky-lit meadows
There sink all fears from fighting your war
Dreaming away tensions for simpler colorations
Sensing serene for sights song

DESPAIR HIDDEN AWAY

Oh God, how I love thy perfection
Yet how very distant I am from its meaning
What a waste your goodness is in me
The waste is not your doing
Only nature's way of making me understand
What I really am

If only I could understand
The distance that holds me so far
From the truth
Or even the appreciation of it
Why do my own faults hold me so aloft?
Even the partial universes
Would not waste their weight
To energize an inefficient body
And even the partial one, truth, and knowledge
Would save his mercy for those who're deserving

To whom does one plea?
For that which should be in her?
A part of the strong being where strength should develop
Where does justice separate from naiveté?
And where does strength separate itself from doubt?

How is well-wishing not adaptive?
How can good intention be worse than conscious wrongdoing?
How can deception be removed from freshness?
And how can a loving soul not be able to love?
And why can love misunderstand?

Why are we animals given emotion
Permitted to feel pain in the soul
If nature intended we only produce
Then why must attachment be so cruel?
What is the use but to give birth and die?

JOY APPROACHING

The essence of what I know as you
Leads me to follow, to understand
There was once a hope, and that was fulfilled
As humanity is, with its ups and downs
So are you shining in beauty?
Intricate and whole
And the average of your giving makes
The happier moments yet more happy
Let yourself shine, and don't let
Your radiance be shadowed by crises
Hold to the sky, so thin, it seems
Yet so vast, so strong, contains a universe
And provides for constant motion of bodies
Can such a prayer be answered
Or must it go unnoticed?

GROWTH OF GOLD

Proud spindles of golden grass
Reaching for the sun to touch
In the drying summer last
Till autumn to be crushed
Bread of life
From golden hills
Penetrating strife
Grow you as God wills

DOUBT OR CONFUSE

My name should have been Thomas
For the doubts I hold in me
I find it hard to realize
That you do truly love me

FOR EASTER

How very simple words can be
And yet how hard I find it
The description of the feeling that I have
Lies only in my soul to be discovered
Easter is the celebration of Jesus, as you said
As you also know, it's more
It's springs rebirth and awakening
I love you and nothing less
Than these sorry words can tell you
I love a man whose heart is dear
And can be warm in this forever
I've never had such drive to say
To express such ancient feelings
And see myself as yet another soul
Lost in the cool air, fainting
Let our bond be born and again reborn
And assure it a steady hold
That secure and dignified in this honor
Will bring us our future and well being
How up in arms my heart is
And dares clasp at yours
That they would cherish each other
And see pain in their separation
Kind man, show me your heart
And your Easter smile
That every morning when the sun is reborn
I can look to the sky and thank him

Spring Melt

I see a streak in the descending snowline
The advance of white crystals for spring dew
Feathered clouds collect about my mountain
Delivering me to the depths of the universe
Moon and starlit space becomes my mood and
I feel the gentleness of a partial heaven
Freedom is never given, but its myth bestows
It is upon me as I am laid to rest in God

QUESTIONS

Even a prayer
Would it reach God?
Prayed from despair
Would he listen at all?
It's only for the good he listens
And let the others fall
For the wise, he glistens
For theirs is true understanding
Of the all

Most mercifully wouldst thou listen
To my plea
That founded in one tear doth read
Call for me and give me peace
In this hour wherein I need

Take from me the dread of what comes
And help me to control what has been done
Help me to follow as I should
And do accordingly as would
The most perfect one.

Disassociated

I took a poem off the wall
And didn't care at all
To care that life should live
Yes, in deep memories
Recall to give
Not to take, to make waste
Leaving the refuse
Another distaste
And there we're to go
Find it traced
To the Creator
Make haste

A Breath

If a breeze were to blow on me like this just a while longer
It would free the dust that clings to me
Like an attic with disuse, cluttered
Filled with debris and spiders working
I've been asleep for so long
Today, for unapparent reason, I woke
On a hopeful thought
A light but serious soul
Praise to one who made this day
That we've had the joy of living it

MY SOUL

It was much like a dream
Where my arms stretched before me
Led the way in my sleep
I felt the floor, walls, and doors
All about me, and yet they weren't there
Or was it me that was away
A departed guest, almost a stranger
But not yet, you (my soul) have taken me back
I can write this now

WANDERING

I would care for more time to speak my mind
I would like to say it, but the words do not form
    As they should, on their own
I must make them, and it distresses me, for I feel
    Weak upon this invitation
A kind of grace from the one who knows all
    In my soul would guide me
Pray let it to me that I may share

THE ESSENCE

What's worst
Waste away the gifts I've failed to discover
The tributes to my maker that lay so dormant
As a winter's sleep with a metabolism low
It keeps my heart from beating
And my body's cold
If the frost would bite me
I would feel its sting
I would feel it in my soul

SHOW ME

Please show me the way
Or that there is a way
That struggles and torments
Are not in vain
And if they are
That they need not be
What is done for rewards?
That bring happiness
Is living for heaven
True desire for life?
Or is living and the desire to know life
The path to heaven?

DEAR GOD LETTER

Dear God
Thank you for this day
For the goodness you have laid upon it
The human within me goes on
Try to appreciate
What is given
While the spirit in me guides me
Beyond this point
Thank you for the joy
We have known through you
For the wonderful times

Lost in an Arbor

Like a flower
The petals fall
One first, and then in synchrony
Others follow
Ever so, they fall
And the beauty is gone
From the bare stem that remains
God! I am not yet there
Still lost
Meandering
Wantonly searching
For an answer
Insight, or simply a sign

Listen Too

I know that the Lord is with me
That he keeps my spirit
That he keeps me in his love
That he shelters me—from the light
That he warms me—from the cold
He gives his righteousness to the world
He gives his love to my brethren
He gives his love
He gives his love
Again he saves me—from the cold
Darkness and the damp cannot kill me
He holds me
He guides my spirit
He guides my life into his heart
He saves us all
He saves us all—from our fears
From our death
The grace he bestows is ours—is ours
Forever and ever—and ever
He keeps me
He loves me
He guides me
That my brothers share my joy
That mourners share my shoulder
They love him, therefore he is theirs
That they love, love one another
God gives them
He gives them
Love eternal
Not persecution
Not dogmatism
He is our solace

LISTEN TOO - 2

Oh, the mighty works of the soul
Unto him!
To him, my soul rises and sings
And calls for its brethren—in God's house
I seek son of him who loves me
Where is the Lord who gave me my life?
Where is the savior of man?
He is responsible for our sorrow and our gilt
No, he's the God who gives us our rights
To live on our own—and fail
But he loves us
He is always there
Clearly, the Lord is ours
Always already the savior
The one who, crèche of God,
Gently rocks us to rest
Yawning in his arms for life
Beyond what we know—what we
What we are able to see
Feeling his arm
We move through the endless universe
God with us
Gently sleeps with us
Praise
      Praise
           Praise
Praise and devotion
To the almighty God
To our praises, he bows his head
He sees our gift
Our hopeless journey
Through this century, we strive
Praise for his attention
To our hearts
Where we fail
Where we neglect the very essence
Of our souls

We succumb to death
Live death
Give unto him who needs us
Give unto him
     Unto him, who dies
And we may give him life
     And yet bring him joy
Amen

LISTEN TOO - 3

Guess who your sufferer in life is
Guess what the sorrow that brings you life is
That the very dying on the cross
The suffering in the desert is but love's token
Love's abiding by your needs
Where the Lord spent
Were the Lord spent
Spent on his labors
His faithful would die
    World dies
    World dies lonely
Go there to the site where
    —when the Lord
    —the Lord stands between
—between the stars
    —between the weary souls
Weary souls watch
For the coming of the verity of eternal kindness
Energy, time, existence
Shown complexity of all matters

WHILE DREAMING

The aspirations of a dark night seem
—seem to grab at my soul
—seem to peel at my heart
Save myself; my song declines to save me
God is there, too, to help us
To help me reach my own reckoning
See the way mountains rise
See the way they all fall as the song that is sung
By living things as they rise
See the song sung in their wake
The sadness of this ring of dawn before the birth of man
Before the dawn

A CHANT - 1

Keep to your warm inner heart
Sings my heart to your soul
Keep your warmth from leaving you die
Some divine graces—
     Give us direction
     Give us your splendor
     Give us the death that
Leads to life everlasting
Amen, amen, dear one
Truth is the divine grace
The existence of my one
Love
Lies in your discovery
Amen

A Chant - 2

Glory be to the Trinity
It is magnified
It is magnified
    In my soul
Soul speak
Speak of the Lord!
Sing of me
Joys that God brings you!
Oh, Holy Spirit
Oh, Holy Father, Spirit, and Son
Oh, holy one
Give us the strength it takes
To live
It is as though we
    Lived in darkness
    Of the world
Oh, Holy Father
Oh, Holy Father
    Spirit
    Give
Spirit, render us your loving
With no religiousness in mind

WISHES AT CHRISTMAS IN INDIA

It doesn't take much to remember
    All these feelings
Warm and solicitous around a small
    Fir tree
When alone you took us in your care
    And
Wished us peace on earth
We wished you
—Goodwill toward men

You sang for us and fed us when
    We longed for
Our loved ones at home, singing us
    Lullabies
Thank you, good people, for your
    Friendship
What all people should be to
    Each other
Whenever, then, and
    Remain
God bless you all, each in your
    Way
Merry wishes, health
    Happiness
Christmas Day!

ABOVE THE TABLE[17]

Rivers run across plains of dust
Eroded and still mystical land
Trees on the inclines of humid slopes
On riverbanks but not flood plains
Was one to wish solutions?
It would be for you
Was one to wish prosperity?
It would be for you
Wish health and all you want
Love only carries wishes

---

17 Poverty exists across all borders, but sometimes it's visible and direct, and we
must reconcile ourselves with what we knew but didn't see then as well as now.
I'm no shining example; these comments were self-directed to a large extent.

But Must Be Active

Taking in hand a future, a path
To run upon
Carrying God's load
Across arid plane
Across roads intersecting
Impoverished villages
To the watering hole
Or wash in Great River

Slimy Tongue
Twister

NIGHT'S-SLIME STORY TALE[18]

Summed: Standing, striding, sliding so smartly, snails: single foot, stomach, stone shell 'n' all, singularly signify selection's satisfaction. Snails are a summitry success, so superbly sublime!

An all-embracing snail, Slips (*snail's name*), slides, and straddles sticks, seldom stuck.

Slime, being a smoothed softener on the sediment's scathed surface, Slips' slime, simulating snow, slides her steadily, similar to a skier's slalom on fluffed, snowy slopes.

Stopping on a sap stem, Slips, slightly slender and "just *starved*," and shining.

She sniffs sedulously and soon spots squirrels speeding, shuffling, and skidding on their creek's summer-cement.

All scooped snacks scattered in sodden soils to store seriously once swept.

Suddenly, a shriek.

SOS. sounds.

Struck by a searing, "Swash!"

Slips stops, scared, so it seems.

Some squirrel had spotted a slick snake—simply a second sooner than it would strike,

---

18 In the illustrated children's version, there is a dictionary for parents. But, who really cares what these sounds say when they're so pleasant to sing? With or without vocabulary, words sing!

... and all squirrels swiftly scurry, anxiously sync—screaming, "Screech!" while signaling swung tails.

Stand! ..."Stomp!" then "Ss-spit!" (of sorts) sounds.

Such a staid step!

Slips sees a spectacularly spotted skunk (not striped skunk).

Its scented spray smell-scarred a sole surreptitious snake, who had scared the two saltating and summit-scaling squirrels.

Slips, so shocked, slides accidentally, her slipper snagging a string.

Slips, "strung up," soiled.

She was slung in a wet straw's swung hammock's sling.

Slips shivers, soft slime's sweat seeps from her molluskan skin.

Semi-seizured and summarily stressed, our shocked Slips seeks silt's shade for silence and slumber.

Soon, Slips' shockwaves soften and succumb to a visionary snail's dreams.

Songs of the saving civil skunk-smell swung her into a sole-slippered dance and supple singer's somnambulant sleep:

> ... stories of sojourns, peerless songs that sole-surviving snails would stout and string,
>
> Slips sings, "So, once was smitten by a scorned snake's cold, scaled scourge and spear ..."
>
> Surely, come a song's stranded stanza's recess ...

Slips' solely opened iris scans

*And sees a surrounding spread of succulent,
unsmeared, sweet swamp's sludge.*

*Slips sets off, dream-striding in the compost's strong,
sovereign soil, twixt rocks along its stone-stippled
stream.*

*With her snail shell swaying, Slips strides along
amidst sounds of forest nightensnails singing.*

She listens, savors, and soon would salivate.

—Apex sapor, copiously scented salads—

*Our singular snail snorts soup, sappy yet simmered;
then pauses.*

*Slips surveys selections sequentially, selecting first
some smeared aspics set in celebrated stone's town
and sunset's summer smorgasbords.*

*The sampled scented spices sequestered from the
superstores were masterful and supine!*

Slips' gastric syrups set off!

*Sediments of hunger's acids send her sensory probosci
spinning, sideways and in circles!*

*And, while sizing up all that was scrumptious in
sleep, Slips' innumerable ravenous instincts strike all
at once!*

Any sounded symphonies cease.

Slips' stellar hypnosis had stopped.

So woken, Slips' soul senses a woken starvation.

Ceaseless, striking "stings" sear her stomach (... a signal from unsweetened and non-syrupy covetous gastric juices craving supper).

Unstuck from the wet straw's hammock's sling and now in soft dry straw, not sleeping, Slips' thoughts swiftly seek something soothing.

She slowly extends outside her snail shell, scanning and surveying her surroundings.

Slips sizes up options, now consciously at last.

"Slide, slurp, snap," Slips' lips and sinuses sing.

Summer's scrumptious suppertime sits near Slip, in sight— requires self-service, of course.

So, responding, now oozing slime and semblant swank, Slips nips the sewn sides of slender sockets of snap peas (slightly sun-seared).

She scarfs all, the small stock's leaves, seeds, and lasting stem, swallowing all smidgens!

Next in sequence come the soft, sumptuous, and sensational s'mores dessert.

Slips' summed s'more consists of a salacious sandwich of scrapped-saltines, white-foamed compote, and slush.

Subsequently, Slips' supper's celestial crest:

Slips' sum absorbs and slurps a sample of the "Snail-on Bleu" silken mycelium sinews, their strands selectively softened and spread over a scorched, fungal, sapphire jelly.

A lasting pleasure spreads inside Slip, throughout.

Slip's sole soul and gastric sphere cast deep sounds, surreally, so satisfied at last.

Slips' siren's sensors summon sleep.

Assuaged and stoic—set in a cedar's shade, her snail eyes sweep a stunning sky.

Soon, she sees a flash.

The transcendent green Saree sweeps swiftly across Slips' summer horizon's silhouette and no sooner had evanesced.

There, softly and soundly, entrusting Slips to a story tale's snail night's soundest sleep.

Biography

In 2006 and 2007, Christine Schonewald's poetry won awards from the San Francisco Writers Conference. *One Stranger's Songs* combines the emotions, observations, inspiration, and humor she's experienced since high school. Born in France, she today lives in the Sierra Nevada foothills as a wife, mother, scientist, professor, and hobbyist (http://www.schonewald.net).